"Each of Don's stories is a small gift. We unwrap them one by one to find inside an unexpected nugget of truth, sweetness and life. His generosity of spirit shines bright between each line about friendship, love and loss to light up the places where we too can be our best selves."

—**Melissa Piasecki, M.D.,** *Professor of Psychiatry, University of Nevada, Reno School of Medicine*

"I feel grateful to have grown up with someone who finds meaning, humor, and perspective in even the small moments of life. Changing with Aging encapsulates these moments and offers heartfelt, bite-size reflections on the human condition. By example, Don Kuhl shows us how to honor pain as much as joy, celebrate failure as much as triumph, treasure people and experiences of all kinds, and continue to grow and play throughout the lifespan. Well done, Dad!"

—**Kate Calhoon, Psy.D.,** *favorite (only) daughter and Licensed Psychologist*

"We all have stories. The best ones make us real to one another. With exquisite vulnerability and hard-earned life wisdom, Don's tapestry of stories is both reflective and informing about the human experience—what helps and what hurts. There is often such exactness of truths that, as I read, I find myself smiling and saying, 'Yes, that's it...that's exactly it.'"

—**Alyssa Forcehimes, Ph.D.,** *President, The Change Companies®*

"I've always admired Don's values and his ability to help and inspire others. It's no surprise he's tackling aging with his wit and humor to help readers face the inevitable (unless we are unfortunate enough to die young)."

—**Karen Gedney, M.D.,** *Author,* 30 Years Behind Bars: Trials of a Prison Doctor

"When you hear the stories Don writes you laugh and then say, 'That's a good story' and then you turn the page to hear another one."

—**Emma,** *6 years*

"Don Kuhl is an incredible and special soul who has committed his life to making a positive difference to so many through his caring and entrepreneurial efforts. This is reflected in his new book, Changing with Aging, *which details his extraordinary journey and will provide inspiration for all who choose to follow in his footsteps. Thank you, Don, for sharing this with the world."*

—**Peter Vegso,** *Publisher, Health Communications, Inc.*

"Don has been a friend and colleague for decades. I am grateful for many things as we age, especially Don's sharing of his stories and vulnerabilities."

—**Stephanie S. Covington, Ph.D., LCSW,** *Co-director, Center for Gender & Justice, La Jolla, CA*

"As someone who finds herself at war with aging, Don's comforting thoughts, new ideas and experiential insights are helping me to embrace the inevitable."

—**Gina Lopez,** *Executive Director, Brewery Arts Center, Carson City*

"There is not one person that won't find themselves in the musings, the essays within Changing with Aging. You will laugh, cry, contemplate, ponder, and reminisce with self. Don Kuhl's style of writing will immediately bring you into not just his life, but the many moments of your own leading to insight, and compassion for self and others. He quickly becomes your friend as you too contemplate the poignant moments of your life's journey."

—**Claudia Black, Ph.D.,** *Author,* It Will Never Happen to Me, *Sr. Fellow, The Meadows*

"Don Kuhl is so frank about aging that his stories sometimes make me wince...and then laugh. But I'm always encouraged. His writing inspires me to grow old gracefully. His clever words and succinct descriptions capture my imagination and challenge me to accept aging with a healthy attitude.

Don is my encouraging friend on this sometimes unnerving path. I no longer feel alone in this whole business of growing older. His stories make me think about things I had never considered. I've learned to laugh or take in stride the changes in my body. His words open my mind to new creativity and help me enjoy my life.

To put it simply, his writing is a delight."

—Jan Raven Stitt

"Don Kuhl's Changing with Aging *reads like a beautiful song. Full of wins, losses, love, joy and laughter, and the wisdom of a life well-lived."*

—Mark Collie, *singer, songwriter, actor*

CHANGING
with
AGING

Little Stories, Big Lessons

by Don Kuhl

Health Communications, Inc.
Boca Raton, Florida

www.hcibooks.com

**Library of Congress Cataloging-in-Publication Data
is available through the Library of Congress**

© 2022 Don Kuhl

ISBN-13: 978-07573-2444-4 (Hardcover)
ISBN-10: 07573-2444-4 (Hardcover)
ISBN-13: 978-07573-2445-1 (ePub)
ISBN-10: 07573-2445-2 (ePub)

HCI, its logos, and marks are trademarks of Health Communications, Inc.

Publisher: Health Communications, Inc.
          1700 NW 2nd Avenue
          Boca Raton, FL 33432-1653

Cover concept design Jenni Hodges
Interior book design Christine Kegel

For Sherry

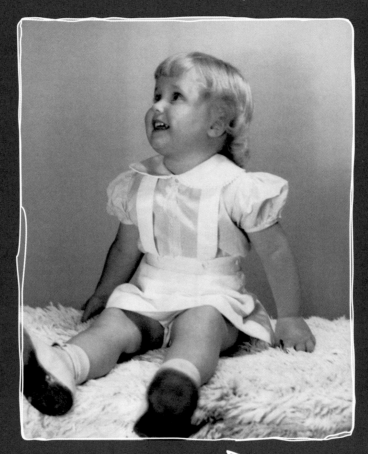

My aging partner

FOREWORD

My friend Don has a time machine. He takes me with him sometimes. You should come, too! Every person who rides in Don's time machine is changed by it.

Health care providers, private corporations and the United States Department of Justice have booked passage on Don's time machine for countless individuals. State and local governments and thousands of rehab centers have booked journeys for people as well. Over 25 million times, Don has helped individuals express and uncover their remarkable selves.

Each trip through time begins with a series of words.

My friend Don is a storyteller.

Stories of the past help us to know who we are.

Stories of the future help us to see who we can become.

Stories are more effective than facts for changing beliefs and behaviors. Facts cause us to put our shields up and become skeptical. But when we are absorbed in a story, we drop our intellectual guard.

With these thoughts in mind, Don invented Interactive Journals, which help people tell their stories and take steps toward their visions for the future.

We imagine every action before we take it. If we want to change our behaviors, we need only to imagine different actions than the ones we have imagined in the past.

Stories are portals of escape into alternate realities.

An examination of the brain of any mammal will let us know its superpower. Monkeys can swing artfully through trees, not because their bodies are different, but because more than half of their brain mass is devoted to depth perception, color differentiation, and guided grasping.

According to Professor Steven Pinker of MIT and Harvard, "The human brain, too, tells a story. Our brains are about three times too big for a generic monkey or ape of our size. The major lobes and patches of the brain are different as well. The olfactory bulbs, which underlie the sense of smell, have shriveled to one third of the expected primate size (already puny by mammalian standards), and the main cortical areas for vision have shrunk proportionally as well...while the areas for hearing, especially for understanding speech, have grown...to twice what a primate our size should have."

The superpower of we humans is our unique ability to attach complex meanings to sounds.

Every word in the English language is composed of just 44 sounds called phonemes. We arrange these into clusters called words which we string together in rapid succession so that others can see in their minds what we see in ours.

Don Kuhl has spent the past 35 years unleashing the power of storytelling in the hearts and minds of millions of people to help them find peace, hope and happiness.

I look forward to seeing where he takes us today.

Roy H. Williams
Founder, Wizard Academy
New York Times *and* Wall Street Journal *bestselling business author,* The Wizard of Ads *trilogy*

CONTENTS

Me. A word from the author

My timeline

We all have one thing in common. We're getting older—and that's a good thing. All these photos are of me. The difference just depends on when you caught up with me.

That's what this book is about. Between these pictures is that stuff called life. Thankfully, most of my life has been a joyous journey—but not always. A blend of my experiences and the wisdom they offered are in the pages ahead.

I hope these stories remind you of your own trip through the years. After all, you could create a similar book, stuffed full of stories, opinions and dreams of your own. If you get in the mood, I'd encourage you to do so. I'd like to read it.

What does your timeline look like?

You can read this book in any way you wish. It's loosely organized in 10 chapters based on lessons I've learned on my journey so far. Feel free to jump to any topic that may have special meaning to you in the moment.

So where did I come from? These two characters. Vern is the one on the right. The power broker is my mother, Irene, before I ever knew her. Like all of us, Irene and Vern aged. In the end, I thought they led pretty complicated and wonderful lives. I fell deeply in love with both of them before they died in 1999, an emotion I failed to share with them for much of their lives. Darn it.

While we're at it, you might as well meet the rest of the family. Take a look at this family picture. The boy praying at the right was my big brother, Eddie. He had a challenging life and died on Christmas day in 2010. Over the years, I loved him and I despised him. Now I miss him.

Next to Eddie is my older sister Connie, the brains of our family and the kindest, most gentle soul I've ever known. She went on to teach at high schools and colleges. I'll bet she was the favorite teacher for hundreds of kids.

The one with her hand on her heart is Marlene, who later changed her name to Kelly. She was a professional dancer who had boys lined up at her door. Kelly never lacks for a point of view, and it's best to agree with her.

Oh, and then there is me. I'm the cute kid on the far left who never liked to stand still for a photo. I still don't.

You'll learn more about all of these folks in the stories that follow.

I'm a dad too. This is Jeff and Kate getting started.

They were sneakier than this photo indicates!

Now they are wonderful adults, halfway through their own aging journeys.

I've traveled through many ups and downs over the years. I was married for 17 years to Jeff and Kate's mother, Kitty, a wonderful woman. Looking back, I think I was a pretty good dad but a terrible husband. I was selfish and inconsiderate and I drank myself to sleep most nights. I was depressed and afraid of tomorrow.

In my 30s, a rough patch landed me at Nova Treatment Center in Oshkosh, Wisconsin. It may have been the most important four weeks of my life. Positive life change is always an option if you want it bad enough. I did.

The next 40 years have been a blessing from above. I married Sherry, one of the best things to happen in my life. You will find her spirit all over the stories that follow.

For seven years, I worked for the University of Wisconsin system and was given unique challenges and opportunities throughout the state. I then became vice president of business development for the parent company of a large healthcare system. All I had learned from my former misadventures came into play. My biggest lesson was to build honest relationships with intelligent people, then shut up and listen to their wisdom.

This led to starting my own company 33 years ago. Initially a tiny, regional publishing company, The Change Companies® now serves over 5,000 clients in all 50 states. My mission in life became clear: to help individuals explore their own life stories and support them in making positive self-change.

What a lucky guy I've been—collecting wonderful friends (human or otherwise), watching my kids become successful and riding the wave of a worthy mission. My journey has allowed me to grow personally and professionally, team up with talented people and give back to my community. This book is my way of sharing my thoughts and experiences along the way. Over the years, I've learned that we all share so much in common. Life is a special gift. Let's make the most of it.

Don Kuhl

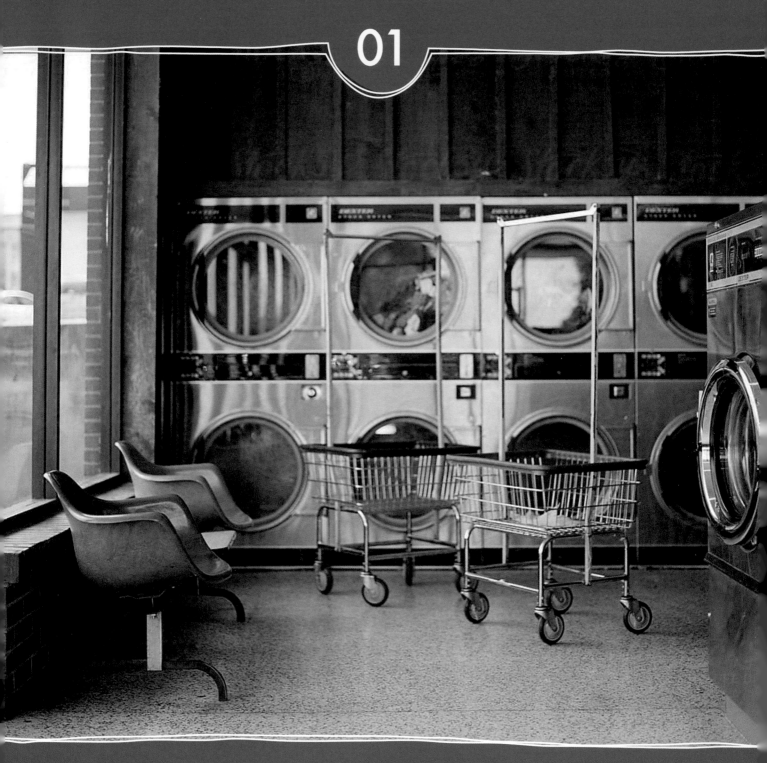

01

Store happy memories in your brain.
Play them often.

At the Laundromat with Dad

Some of my most embarrassing moments while in high school happened while I was forced by my mother to join my dad, Vern, in doing the weekly laundry. It included all the dirty underwear for the entire family. Of course, the laundromat was located right across the street from a malt shop and record store, popular hangouts for girls in my class I was trying to impress.

Vern wasn't too happy about the task either and sweated profusely just waiting for a dryer to open up. Socks went missing. Coin machines jammed. Vern and I faced off, folding sheets. He shook them hard, and the corners slipped from my fingers. Clean, damp linen hit dirty linoleum. Vern started to say nasty words but remembered our location and just uttered sounds, like a squirrel caught in a cage.

My greatest fear was realized when Pam Hawkins, a girl so pretty I was afraid to look up at her when we passed in the school cafeteria, was staring across at us from the record store. For the first time, she recognized me, smiled and waved. I think I was holding one of my sister's Wonderbras.

I negotiated a date with Pam Hawkins my senior year!

Many years later, when my dad moved in with Sherry and me, we laughed about those awkward trips to the laundromat. Most bonding between fathers and sons took place at baseball games or fishing trips. Our bond was Tide Clean.

Poncer Dog

Sherry and I bought our first pup, Ponce de Leon, in Dayton, Nevada, at a defunct pet store that was being turned into a pizza place. We closed the deal with a $20 bill and our lives changed forevermore.

I could write a book about the misadventures of "Poncer Dog" and how the speckled puppy with tiny legs and a barrel chest captured our love for a decade. However, this brief story is all about how stirring up memories can be more effective than an aspirin.

Monday was a tough day. One of our employees made a silly and costly error. I learned an old friend died of a heart attack. My new cellphone did not listen to my commands. I got on the scale and found I had gained three pounds on my new diet. I opened my truck's glove compartment and discovered a nest of little mice. I told Sherry she was in a bad mood (not a good idea on any day).

So what does a blue Monday have to do with a mutt who died 15 years ago? I've learned all I need to do is lay on my back, take a few deep breaths, close my eyes and see that darn puppy's floppy ears coming toward me. I can feel his cool nose on my cheek. I whisper, "Hi, little fella," and I feel a jolt of joy.

I believe we all have our Ponce de Leons in our memory bank. We just need to call for them.

Store happy memories in your brain. Play them often.

august. 1935

My mother was full of gumption.

Irene Duffy Kuhl

My mother was full of gumption. On the first day I remember her, Irene Duffy Kuhl was soaping up the back of the bathtub so I could slide down it. She was still showing off her gumption the hour she died as she complimented a nurse on her "beautiful blue uniform," while letting her know the chicken soup at lunch was a little too salty.

Irene worked at banks for most of her 89 years. Her title was executive secretary, but she acted as if she was president of The La Grange State Bank. Many clients and employees may have thought she was, too. Brimming with confidence and competence, she was known by most of the "important people" in our Chicago suburb.

But I knew her most as mom. She made each of her four children feel very special. I was her youngest and grew up with lots of love. However, Irene Duffy had high expectations for each of her children, too. We all had part-time jobs by the time we were nine, and every penny went into our personal accounts at her bank. I failed at numerous things as a kid, but hearing my mom describe my accomplishments to anyone who would listen, I was a superstar. She convinced me I was, which had both its upsides and downsides.

Irene Duffy Kuhl died on May Day of 1999. I've thought of her every day since. As I age, I recognize the significant role my mom played in each year of my life. Only recently do I give her full credit for the good that came to me through her love and gumption. At the same time, I take personal responsibility for those areas in which I fell short of Irene's expectations.

Unhandy Man

All my life, I've been known as the unhandy man. My reputation was etched into the memories of friends and family many years ago.

It happened when a seldom-used toilet kept running. I inspected the back tank and discovered when I pulled up on the little black bobber, the leaking stopped.

Then inspiration hit. I took my third place bowling trophy and set it down in the tank with the bowling arm strategically placed under the metal bar attached to the black bobber. The fit was perfect, the toilet was cocked for one good flush and the leaking noise was gone.

All I needed to do was reset my contraption after each flush.

It worked for weeks. Then a visiting friend, who happened to be a retired plumber, got an upset stomach and chose to double flush. My nosy friend opened the back tank and pulled out my bowling trophy. My ingenuity quickly spread throughout the neighborhood.

A big piece of aging is to remember and enjoy all the silly stuff you did in your younger days. For me, creative toilet repair remains toward the top of my list.

Four Big Boulders

The first home Sherry and I purchased was a tiny one. It sat on a dusty lot. It was all we could afford, and we loved every square foot. On Sundays, we took off to the desert in our 1971 Oldsmobile Delta 88 (purchased for $200) to search for stupendous boulders to decorate our yard. Among hundreds of rocks we retrieved, four were special. Each one weighed at least 100 pounds, and it took all our might to hoist them up and into the trunk of our Olds.

We placed them in prominent spots around our house. On tough days, we would pat our colorful boulders for luck before heading off to work.

Twenty-five years and several homes later, I remembered the four big boulders and went back to our old house to see if I could purchase them as a surprise gift for Sherry's 70th birthday.

The owner of the house must have sensed the sentimental value I placed on the four rocks and knew a sucker had just rung his doorbell. His price was $250 per boulder.

Later that day, when Sherry walked up our driveway and spotted our four favorite boulders, she giggled wildly and then teared up with joy as she patted each one of her old buddies.

Pound for pound, it was the best thousand bucks I ever spent.

Best Seat in Town

My favorite Christmas gift was not receiving the present "Santa" had planned to put under the tree.

I was five years old and my dad, Vern, whispered to me that he heard a rumor from up North that Santa was considering giving me my own Schwinn bike.

I started to cry and uttered, "I don't want a bike for Christmas! That Santa can stick it back on his sleigh."

Poor Vern was dumbfounded and must have taken the news back to Mrs. Claus, Irene, to figure things out.

Early Christmas morning, I rushed down the stairs to find a cool, electric train zipping around the tree. I was full of joy. No Schwinn.

The story behind the story? I loved to ride on my brother, Eddie's handlebars. It was the best seat in Ames, Iowa. It made us a dynamic duo, and it proved Eddie's love for me.

The following August, on my birthday, I received the bright red Schwinn that had been hidden up in the attic. At age six, I was ready to pedal on my own. And Eddie helped me stay upright for the next few years.

Eddie died in 2010.
I miss him so much.

My Prospects

Some romances that last for decades begin in the strangest ways.

That happened to me.

I've always been a sales guy of some sort. Nearly 30 years ago, I was practicing my trade in Madison, Wisconsin. The fancy spot to eat lunch was the Madison Club, right off the square. Legislators, business leaders and university professors would head there to eat and conduct the business of the day.

I'd bring in my prospects and focus on closing a sale before leaving the table.

The waitress would take our order and perfectly serve each of my guests. However, I would never receive what I ordered. Instead, I'd get a dish full of healthy food—certainly not my choice of the day.

I'd say nothing. I was closing a deal. My guests never noticed. They were too busy eating a prime rib sandwich with fries, while I stared down at bean sprouts.

This went on for months. Then one day, a warm piece of chocolate cake topped with French vanilla ice cream was placed before me.

I looked up at the waitress. She smiled.

We married 14 months later.

Wearing Dad's Watch

My watch tells me what time it is—and who I am.

The watch is an ACQUA Indiglo, and it belonged to my father, Vern. He wore it for many years as a salesperson crossing Midwestern states in search of high-rising grain elevators needing aeration systems. It was with great pride that he gave it to me shortly before he died in 1999. I've worn it ever since, often driving down the same roads my father did. Deep down we were both salesmen, my dad closing deals with farmers and me pitching to hospital administrators. Vern taught me a bunch about sales, honesty and embracing life as a roadway to travel and enjoy.

When possible, it's important to me to touch the belongings of people I love, who shaped the person I am today. I remember when my dad took off his watch, his berry-brown wrist had a white-flesh brand in the shape of his timepiece. I think of him every time I remove my watch and see the same brand.

Today, eBay has an ACQUA Indiglo watch on sale for eight dollars.

My watch is priceless.

Rock Solid

When I first moved west, I was taken by the beautiful rocks all over the place. As a unique gift to my parents back in Pennsylvania, I found a smooth stone with streaks of gold and blue and green. I wrapped it up in a white, silk cloth, put it in a gold box and sent it off.

Every time I visited my folks, I'd smile when finding my rock on my mom's favorite glass table, right next to the Hummel figurines she loved so much.

In 1999, when both my mom and dad passed, Sherry and I went through the "treasures" they left behind. I spotted the gold box in which I had shipped out the beautiful rock. Taped on top of the box, in my mother's distinguished handwriting, was a note: "Stick this rock on the table when Don visits."

Some people may consider this an example of trickery. I consider it an act of tenderness from a mother who loved her youngest boy.

I had a front row seat to some of the grittiest shows that never made it to the screen.

La Grange Theatre

Sixty years ago, my bedroom window looked out on the back wall of The La Grange Theatre. As a kid, I had a great view of everything happening in a suburban Chicago alleyway.

On the other side of the red brick wall, movies were being shown featuring the stars of the day: Marilyn Monroe, Jimmy Stewart, Joan Crawford. Some of the popular movies were "Ben-Hur," "Some Like It Hot" and "The Diary of Anne Frank." I didn't see many of the movies, but I viewed a lot of the real action back in the alley.

Attractions included:

A "smokin" hot romance between a teenage boy and a lady about twice his age. The lighting wasn't great, but I think they both were having a fine time.

A brief fight. One swing, and the bigger man went down. He chose to stay there. I thought he was smart.

An exchange of a paper bag for a fistful of dollars. They seemed to be in a hurry. I didn't think it was popcorn.

An old fella with a bottle of wine wrapped in a brown sack. He just sat there on a cement block, sipping his beverage. He made many repeat performances.

I could go on and on. There may have been some fine acting on the big screen inside the La Grange Theatre. But I had a front row seat to some of the grittiest shows that never made it to the screen.

Love Me Tender

Certain little moments of joy stay with me for my lifetime.

Jerry Dahl was a grade school buddy who lived about 10 blocks from Saint Cecilia School. I'd walk him home and go up to his room, which was in the attic. As with many Catholic families of the '50s, Jerry had a bunch of siblings. One of them was Judy, who was a few years older and the romantic target of my brother Eddie.

One afternoon, Jerry swiped a 45 record from his sister's room of my brother breathlessly singing the Elvis Presley hit "Love Me Tender" and dedicating it to his undying affection for Judy. I had discovered a gold mine.

That evening at dinner, I mixed Eddie's remake of "Love Me Tender" with other 45 records that would automatically flop down on our RCA record player. As the baked beans were being passed, Eddie's whispered words filled the kitchen: "This is for you, Judy." What followed was my brother's humble efforts to sing one of Elvis's greatest hits.

Speaking of hits, I was pummeled that evening when Eddie caught up with me in the backyard. No matter the temporary pain, this caper remains one of my most joyous moments.

Bygone Days of Dictionaries

Kids don't need to learn to spell anymore. That's what Google and Bing are for.

However, on my desk is a copy of *Webster's New Practical Dictionary* from 1951.

It belonged to my mother, who used it daily as a secretary at the Ames Trust and Savings Bank. On the blank yellowed front pages are handwritten words a young Irene Kuhl had trouble spelling: reminiscence, Albuquerque, pamphlet, Cincinnati, analysis.

What's wrong with me? Well into the 21st century, I keep using an outdated dictionary that is right next to my new Apple computer. It's amazing how often the word I'm uncertain of is right there in front in my mother's beautiful longhand.

I'm such a sap. Last night I felt a tear in my eye when Irene Kuhl reminded me that "occurred" has two cs and two rs.

Connie

That's me!

Connie's Love

Connie just turned 80. She's my big sister, and I love her.

When I was a grade school kid, Connie woke me up in the dark. We walked our golf bags a mile to the golf course before it opened. Nine holes later, Connie left for work. I went back to bed.

Connie was the brightest of Vern and Irene's four children. She won all kinds of scholarships and stuff. She collected close friends at Ames High School as easily as I collected lightning bugs.

Once, my brother Eddie was beating me up pretty bad. Connie came to my rescue, hitting Eddie with her left hand while biting her own right forearm. She wanted to make sure she was hurting herself more than she was hurting my brother.

As a frightened and confused teenager, I left home and hitchhiked from Chicago to "I don't know where." Cold, broke and afraid, I wound up at Connie's apartment on Arapahoe Street in Denver, Colorado. After a few days, she sent me in the right direction.

I hope everyone has a sister as good as Connie. But I bet it's pretty rare.

For your grandchildren's sake, please journal a bit about what you did today.

Hank

My dad's dad, Hank, died in 1932, 13 years before I was born.

A year before my dad died in 1999, I asked him to journal about Hank. To my surprise, he did. Here are tidbits of a few of his wonderful stories.

"In the spring of '25, an airplane flew over the schoolhouse, and the teacher, Miss Yegge, told all the students to run out and see the passing fancy because the Bible said only birds were meant to fly. The kids all agreed with Miss Yegge."

"One day, when my mom was ill, she ordered Hank to go to town and buy bread. At the prospect of paying a quarter for three loaves, Hank was upset and stated that a family that had to buy bread (rather than bake it) would surely end up in the poor house."

"When the Ogden, Iowa, fairgrounds were converted to a golf course, Hank told me he hoped I would have better things to do in my life than chase a little white ball around a pasture."

These are all gifts that my father, Vern, gave me about Hank. Today, I fly around the country, play golf and buy bread. But I fell in love with Hank.

For your grandchildren's sake, please journal a bit about what you did today.

Floating on the Skunk River

The South Skunk River flooded the driving range when I was 11.

It took me out of my golf ball picker-upper job for six days. But it was grand.

Floyd Penkhus, my boss, let Steve, the Hedberg boys and me use his red rowboat, and off we went. We took a left at the 225-yard marker and explored uncharted territories of Ames, Iowa.

Steve had stashed 50 cherry bombs from the Fourth of July. I swiped a whole box of Hostess cupcakes from the pantry, and Gene Hedberg brought a mammoth jug of A&W root beer.

We were explorers and conquistadors of the highest order. We threw cherry bombs in the muddy water and watched them explode. We guzzled root beer and stuffed our mouths with the chocolate cupcakes. We took turns rowing, bumping into trees that dotted our wilderness. We sang, "Davy, Davy Crockett, king of the wild frontier." Life was super.

At 74 years of age, I try to recapture those pure moments of joy. I play with my four shepherds in our creek. I hike up the mountainside and spot a pack of coyotes down below.

And when things are just right, I sing boldly to nobody, "Born on a mountaintop in Tennessee."

Risk Taking

I've always been a risk taker.

When I was a freshman in high school, I took my first commuter train ride into downtown Chicago. A friend had told me I could buy a magazine full of pictures of "pretty girls" at a drug store on State Street.

There I was, at age 14, in a strange, big city searching for forbidden fruit. I found the drug store. For appearance's sake, I stood in line holding a *Chicago Tribune*, three packs of gum, a tube of Pepsodent toothpaste and the aforementioned magazine. The old fella behind the counter smiled, rang up all my other items but held on to the magazine.

I got lost and scared before getting on the wrong commuter at the train station. I wound up in a Chicago suburb, 40 miles from home, clutching my bag with the tube of Pepsodent inside.

As an elder gentleman, I still take risks. However, now I don't have my dad to call to get me home safely.

There is valor in defeat if the cause is noble.

A Good Fight

Darwin Slocum put up a hell of a battle.

It was the early 1980s, and the tiny University of Wisconsin campus in Medford was attempting to stay open. It was the smallest campus of 27 that made up the University of Wisconsin system. I was dispatched from the central office in Madison to assist Dean Slocum in the final, futile effort to keep serving the 90-plus students and the little community of Medford in the tradition of The Wisconsin Idea: the boundaries of the university are the boundaries of the state.

Late one night, I remember having a beer with Darwin at The Tombstone Tap (home of the original Tombstone Pizza). He told stories of students who had begun their education in Medford and went on to graduate with honors at the Madison campus. He pulled a program out of his vest pocket from a production of "The Music Man," which had drawn packed audiences five nights in a row.

His eyes glistened. "The board of regents must recognize our county needs this campus."

I already knew the battle was over. Only one member of the board was in favor of keeping the doors open.

But I recognized there is valor in defeat if the cause is noble.

"Darwin," I said, "let's keep fighting for Medford." We did.

The buildings were shuttered three months later.

It's so simple. Future generations will be just fine.

My Picture for the Future

Sometimes a picture explodes in my mind that's too wondrous to let pass. This was one of them.

I'm driving in Carson City on Arrowhead Road to the office. I just returned from a stressful two-day meeting in Salt Lake City. I'm not exactly depressed—well, maybe just a bit.

Then I spot them. A grandma with a big sun hat, sitting on a stool and staining a wood fence. On the other side of the fence is a boy, maybe seven, who has a brush in his little hand. Most of his brown paint is landing on the grass below the fence or on his previously white tennis shoes.

They are talking. They are laughing. It's a fabulous scene of Americana. I rush to my office to get Michelle, our photographer, so I can capture this scene for the rest of my life.

It's so simple. Future generations will be just fine.

How do I know?

A grandmother is with her grandson, laughing, talking and painting their fence a loving shade of brown.

Under the Lights

My first football game under the big lights took place on Curtiss Street in Ames, Iowa.

It was Irene and Vern's bridge night across town. Big brother Eddie had a master plan. I was about seven but "very gifted" for my age. Eddie told me to collect every lamp in the house and bring them out to the front yard. Eddie started collecting electrical cords from our house and the neighborhood's open garages.

Within an hour, a lighted football field was in place. The yard lines were marked by three cans of my father's shaving cream. The most talented kids from blocks around were chosen for action. Other kids lined the field to create a growing crowd of spectators. Billy Wilson provided play-by-play broadcasting using his sister's hairbrush as a microphone.

The game was cut short—but not before the living room floor lamp crashed to the turf and my mom's favorite table lamp fell prey to an errant pass. An older couple across the street squealed on us.

Irene and Vern arrived about the same time as Officer Flynn. The field went dark.

At 76, the memory still makes me smile.

Holding Hands

As an old guy, I still love to hold the hand of the woman I love.

However, I had a tough start.

Mary Watson was special in seventh grade. She could twirl a baton better than most of the high school girls. When I was lucky, I'd see Mary walking home after band practice, and I'd walk alongside. My plan was to reach down and hold her hand for the final block to Doctor Watson's residence.

I'd practiced for this moment. I'd used my own hands to see if a finger interlocking grip was preferred over a simple palm on palm technique. I practiced the line, "Hey, let's hold hands just for the fun of it." How stupid is that? Experienced, confident hand holders would just go for it.

My time came. Mary's baton was in her off hand. Maybe Mary was giving me the green light. Right in front of her door, I finally grabbed for her free hand. Startled, Mary pivoted. Her baton hit me square in the nose. Blood trickled from my right nostril. Dr. Watson opened the front door. A light beamed out. I made a run for it before Dr. Watson could offer me medical assistance.

Things have gotten better. Sherry and I hold hands a lot.

Sherry likes the palm on palm technique. I'm good with that.

02

Stay silly.

Don't miss an opportunity to play.

Gin Rummy

I'm not saying there aren't a lot of exciting, romantic moments as Sherry and I cement our relationship well into our 70s—but the glue that holds it all together is gin rummy.

We play every day—often several times a day. Our first game begins before 6 a.m. We sip coffee, eat our eggs and ham, and shuffle the cards.

Every game goes to 1,000 points, which takes the better part of a week. I know I am the better player, but the score often does not support my assumption.

We have strict rules. During competition, we can call each other horrific names with no later repercussions. During the heat of battle, our creative use of adjectives would embarrass a sailor.

Another rule is, if we get dealt a terrible hand, either one of us can throw our cards at the face of our adversary and demand a reshuffle. This aggressive action can only be taken one time per sitting.

You may think keeping an exciting marriage together is best achieved by sharing a fine bottle of wine, snuggling close together by an open fire, or even surprising your spouse with roses or candy.

Nope. The magic is a daily jolt of gin rummy.

Recess

I love to play. I always have, first as a little kid, playing kick the can and tag and knocking on my friend Billy's door asking if he could come out and play. As a teenager I played with basketballs and baseballs, and as a father I played often with my eager children. As I'm aging, I'm finding it harder and harder to find playmates. No one is interested in following me out the back door. They say they are too busy or it's too warm or too cold outside or they have two bad knees.

That doesn't stop me. I still shoot free throws, pretending the game's in overtime, or throw a baseball in the air and act like it's a high pop fly. I face off in tennis against the garage door and throw the football through the tire swing long abandoned by my grandchildren.

Where's Billy when I need him?

Ping-pong Prank Parting

I put glue on Bob Thompson's side of the ping-pong table during our last contest. The ball just stuck there, and I did a victory dance around his living room. It was two weeks before he died of congestive heart failure.

Years earlier, I worked for Bob when he headed a campus at the University of Wisconsin and students broke into his office the night before his 60th birthday and filled it from floor to ceiling with balloons. They loved their dean.

Bob and I used to go to garage sales in Chicago on Saturday mornings to see who could buy the stupidest item for the lowest price. He was a great negotiator.

Bob Thompson recommended me for a position at the university, for which I was vastly underqualified. Magically, I got the job.

I drove 380 miles in a snowstorm to play that last game of ping-pong with my dying friend and mentor. At the end of the contest, we laughed, looked each other in the eyes and hugged for the last time.

It was the best trip I will ever make.

As you age, don't ever miss saying goodbye to your Bob Thompsons.

Sherry encouraging
me to dance

Boogie On

If I had to do life all over again, I'd be an accomplished dancer. I wouldn't specialize in just one type of dance, I'd be good at them all: ballet, tap, rock, modern, salsa, waltz and hip-hop.

Then, at our recent holiday party, when this popular dance band encouraged guests to get out on the dance floor, I'd be confidently saying to myself, "Bring it on!" Next, I'd be roaming the tables beckoning various shy, but willing, ladies to join me. I wouldn't care what song the band was playing; I could dance to them all. Everyone would surround the dance floor and start to slowly clap to the beat of the music. At the end of each dance, I'd graciously bow to my partner as if all compliments should go her way.

Actually, I was in the back corner of the room, snacking on chips and cheese dip and engaging a few other non-dancing male friends in banter about bitcoins, of which I know nothing about.

Later, at home with Sherry, who is exhausted from her boogie-full evening, I take off my shirt and look in the mirror. I slowly rotate my stomach to the left and then to the right. I tell her, "Yes, I think belly dancing is for me."

King Kong

I do three simple things at once that always make me feel happier, healthier and more connected with my neighbors.

The first is recommended by almost every expert in healthcare. I go for a walk—for me, it's down Franktown Road in Washoe Valley. My physical condition limits the length and the speed of my walk, but that's okay. The key is to get out the door and put one foot in front of the other.

The second thing I do is bounce a red Kong ball—the round, bouncy version of the famous dog toy. It's a great ball I can bounce from one hand to the other with each step. I have also developed several sophisticated bounce patterns which take special skill and practice—and often force me to retrieve the Kong ball from the side of the road.

The third thing is the most important. As cars go by, I smile and wave at the drivers. My rough study indicates nearly 80 percent of the drivers smile and wave back. The other 20 percent are having a bad day.

A happy and healthy life can be a ball.

Women wave at a 30% greater rate than men. Must be my good looks!

Don, Joe and Harry

I've been going to the same grocery store for over 10 years, often having the pleasure of Amy helping me bag my groceries. When I first met Amy, I could tell she was struggling with her job, but she stayed with it. Frequent customers were kind and patient, even if the line backed up a bit.

After about a year, Amy had memorized my name, so she began to greet me by saying "Hi Joe" or "Hi Harry." We would look at each other and have a good laugh and then Amy, without fail, would tap me on the shoulder and smile and say, "I know your real name is Don." This routine went on for years.

Recently, I've missed seeing Amy. Last week, the store manager told me she turned in her resignation for personal health reasons.

I'll still go to the same market, but I really miss being called Joe or Harry and having a good laugh.

My Rock Star Stage

I have a great idea for older folks who, like me, can't sing a lick.

I have this little hike I go on that gets me away from everybody. Up there, rising above the sagebrush, is a big flat rock about three feet off the ground. One day, while sitting on the rock, I had this great urge to burst out into song. I looked around, took a deep breath and began to shout out my mother's favorite song, "Oh, Danny boy, the pipes, the pipes are calling..."

It sounded good—too good. Almost like it wasn't coming from me but from the rock. I continued to bellow, "From glen to glen and down the mountainside..." I wasn't sure of the words, but I couldn't stop. "The summer's here and the flowers are growing big..." A jackrabbit darted for cover, but I didn't care. I'm a rock star.

Since this first discovery I have secretly extended my repertoire to include "Yesterday" (Beatles) and "Candle in the Wind" (Elton John).

So now I have a little musical haven of my own where "I've Gotta Be Me" (Sammy Davis Jr.) and no one thinks "I'm Crazy" (Patsy Cline).

I Spy

I don't want you to get the impression I sneak around following people all day, but once in a while I do enjoy watching folks' movements when they don't know I'm tracking them.

Today was one of those days. I was floating around Costco, checking out free food samples. Sherry was doing some serious shopping, which I wanted no part of. So, I spotted this couple, maybe in their early 70s, laughing and skipping along like two silly teenagers.

If you've been to Costco, you know this was a very weird encounter. Most couples are pushing carts with huge supplies of dog food, frozen vegetables and toilet paper. They don't appear joyous. More likely, a fight is about to commence as soon as they get to the privacy of their vehicles.

I followed this cock-a-hoop couple up and down the aisles. My curiosity was piqued. How could they be having so much fun? When they looked my way, I cleverly pretended to be searching for breakfast cereal.

Holy smokes! I discovered their secret. These senior citizens were taking little packages of personal hygiene items and slipping them into the carts of unsuspecting shoppers.

I wanted to rush over and give them each a big hug.

I thought, this is what aging should be all about.

Hat Trick

I purchased a cowboy hat for our corporate Christmas party being held at an old hotel in Virginia City. It cost me $150. I've purchased two suits with matching ties for less than that.

The moment I put it on my head in this authentic western store, I knew it was meant for me.

For nearly thirty years, I've felt like a transplant from Madison, Wisconsin, living in "Bonanza" country. It's as if I hadn't earned my "spurs" to play like a real westerner. Yet, when I put on this hat, my whole life changed. I looked down at my loafers and knew it was time for some real cowboy boots. I checked out leather vests and red bandanas. The theme song of "Rawhide" came whistling through my ears.

I got totally lost in the moment. I strutted outside to find my horse for the ride back to Washoe Valley.

Instead, my 2009 blue Chevy Suburban was in my parking space.

Partners, when you get up there in years, it's okay to frolic in your dreams.

I crumpled up my parking ticket, hopped into my Suburban and quietly said, "Giddy-up."

When you get up there in years, it's okay to frolic in your dreams.

Racing Waldo

One of the greatest inventions of all time is the Slinky. Richard James must have been a fun guy. He invented my favorite toy back in the 1940s.

This morning, after completing a few stretching exercises, I'm at the top of the stairs. Next to me, ready for competition, is Waldo, my Slinky.

The winner is whoever can get down the stairs first.

Years ago, I beat Waldo all the time. I'd be waiting for Waldo at the bottom of the stairs as he lackadaisically slinked along.

Either Waldo has picked up his game, or, surprisingly, I'm a tad bit slower.

While safely clutching the handrail, I say, "Ready... set..."—and I take off while Waldo is waiting for my "...go."

I'm not cheating. I just want to win.

Waldo passes me on the sixth stair.

Photo Shoot

Every four years or so, I'm invited to do a photo shoot at the Department of Motor Vehicles. I believe they fly in a professional photographer from one of those studios in Los Angeles to make certain they capture my total essence.

I thought the COVID-19 lockdown might discourage the power brokers from bringing in the best, but sure enough, last week I showed up at the DMV and there was supermodel photographer Wilma Fairbanks. After Joe Easton gave me a vision test and asked me a few questions, I was royally escorted over to Wilma's studio.

She told me to stand on this special taped line on the floor and look straight into the camera.

"Should I give it my famous smile?" I inquired.

"Just stand still and quit squinting," Wilma replied playfully.

I heard a click and saw the flash. Magic was in the air.

Eight days later, I received the final photographic masterpiece in the mail. My portrait even included my height, my weight and an encouragement to wear my glasses whenever I drive.

Can the life of an aging star get any better than this?

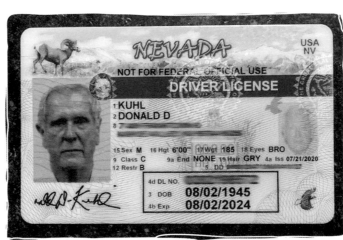

The Eleventh Commandment

Young kids and old men have something in common. If they have an ingenious trick to pull off, they don't get too concerned about the consequences.

One of my best stunts in grade school was with my buddy, Super Steve. We were playing football on the playground, and Super Steve kicked the ball onto the flat roof of the school. After the Big Ten Commandments, commandment number 11 at St. Cecilia's was, "Thou shalt never climb up on the school roof."

But a ladder was close at hand and (it appeared to us) no one was looking. As we started the forbidden climb, Monsignor Ryan came storming out of the rectory and demanded our descent.

He scolded us unmercifully, either using the Lord's name in vain or reciting an unfamiliar prayer featuring the Big Guy. He tweaked our ears and slapped the backs of our heads. Monsignor Ryan proceeded to climb the ladder to retrieve our football.

Super Steve and I looked at each other. Then smiled. We removed the ladder from the side of the school and ran like hell.

At age 75, I'm always on watch for similar opportunities.

I paid a price from Vern that evening...ouch!

Blue

I can't get rid of my old, faithful 2009 Chevy Suburban. I bought it used over a decade ago. Early on, I lost it in a big parking lot, so I got a cheap new paint job. I chose the most unique shade of blue imaginable so it would stick out from other vehicles in all circumstances.

It only took me a few days after that to fall in love with the car. I pretend my Suburban has a brain and a heart. I named it Blue, for obvious reasons. In frigid weather, when I leave a restaurant or store, I call out, "Come, Blue!" as if my Suburban will fire up and rush to the door. It doesn't, of course. Adults think I'm a little loco, but kids keep waiting to see if Blue will hustle to me.

I've been in the little town of Carson City for nearly 30 years. Lots of town folks know me, and most of them like me—I think. I don't lock Blue up when I go to the grocery store or shopping mall. Often, when I return to Blue, a friend—or even a whole family—will be sitting inside, waiting to say hello. Blue likes it. And so do I.

I'm confident Blue will stay with me until I drop dead. And who knows? Shortly thereafter, I'll shout out, "Come, Blue!" and my faithful Suburban will whisk me away to a fantastic destination.

I'm a Winner

To win in life, it helps to get comfortable with losing. I have a tip: Always find someone better than you to challenge. For me, it's a natural talent.

As a younger man, I worked for a year on the Sheboygan Campus of the University of Wisconsin. I thought I was a good tennis player. Then, I met Sandy, a young co-ed who was barely five feet tall. We got into the habit of playing a set of tennis at lunch. A crowd would gather—Sandy's boyfriends. My plan was to play my strong game, overpower her, rush to the net. It would be a part of her higher education. This is when I learned what a lob in tennis is all about. I never won a single game against Sandy. However, I did learn how to accept crowds of people snickering without a sense of humiliation.

This was not the first or last time I discovered how easy it is for me to lose. My older years have provided numerous opportunities. My grandson Carter can whip me at HORSE, even on my home court. My friend Larry waits for me at the finish line after a run around Spooner Lake. My wife, Sherry, beats me at every game we play (and we play a lot of games).

My opinion? Coming in first isn't what counts. Playing the game is what makes you a winner.

Storm is a-Brewing

It's not rare for high winds, rain and snow to whip over the Sierra mountaintops and descend on Washoe Valley. When this happens, Sherry and I attempt to "batten down the hatches" around our property. Lawn chairs are put up against the house, away from windows. Garbage cans are placed safely in the garage, and yard supplies are secured in the tool shed.

Here's the weird part. Sherry and I put on our tough-weather clothes and head outside, our four white Swiss shepherds at our sides. Often, we need to wrap our arms around a tree, or each other, so we don't get toppled over. Sillier yet, we have been known to sing "God Bless America" at the top of our lungs as our neighbor's plastic swimming pool flies above us and loose shingles disengage from nearby rooftops.

What's wrong with us? We have been doing this thing for over 30 years. We've never been dealt a serious blow, although our sanity has been questioned by many a neighbor.

The answer rests with the word "exhilaration." We love the feelings of elation, excitement and happiness. They beat out moderate risk and mockery from timid neighbors every time.

I've got to go. Black clouds are looming over Slide Mountain.

03

Give love.
Hang on to your most meaningful relationships.

Enduring Friendships

Rarely do people ask me for advice.

But recently, at a meeting with young business men and women in Reno, I was asked to share one thing I would do differently over the last 30 years.

Since this was a rare occasion, I didn't want to mess up my answer. So I pondered the question for a few moments.

Then I said something close to this: "I'd find ways to keep my true friends attached to me forever."

They may have wanted something more profound, but that's what they got.

Why?

I've squandered a few true friends who were loyal and honest and brought me joy and peace. Often the losses were caused by a move to another city, a change in careers or a silly disagreement over insignificant matters.

Now, in my mid-70s, I realize there are few things more precious than people who are kind and patient enough to discover the genuine me and fully accept what they see.

Give love. Hang on to your most meaningful relationships.

Frank's Trick

My best friend of all times was 30 years older than me. His name was Frank, and he was a mentor to me in so many ways long before the term "life coach" came into popularity.

As a current old geezer at 73, I feel a tug of obligation to pass on a trick Frank played on me when I was young and a bit bewildered.

Frank always acted as if I had already achieved a positive trait or skill I was struggling to attain. He treated me as if I were wiser than I truly was. He assumed I was acting in a noble, unselfish manner long before it dawned on me to do so.

It put a lot of pressure on me to be the guy Frank already had christened me as being. I'm a better man today because Frank saw a beauty in me long before I caught up with his positive image.

Many years after Frank has passed, I try to pull the same trick on young people I love.

Just Listen

As I age, I think I grow smarter about who I choose to spend time with. If I could go back in time, I believe I would chase after folks who could mentor me on getting wiser and kinder each day. Those people were all around me, but I think they scared me off. I was worried they would find out what a loser I really was. Instead, I hung out in bars searching for patrons who might think I was pretty special.

It took me more years than it should have to recognize how many great people were all around me. I didn't need to impress them. I just needed to listen to them.

Memory Loss

Scott Stanley may have saved my marriage...my second one. He's a friend and a research professor at The University of Denver who specializes in studying relationships.

I thought I was an expert at retelling conversations of the past to win heated arguments. Not only did I believe I had instant recall of what I had said two weeks or 10 years ago, but I also believed I had instant recall of precisely what my loved one had said, as well. With this great power, I thought I could slant any argument in my favor.

It never worked. Even when I thought I won the skirmish, I had a hunch I was losing the relationship.

Dr. Stanley said, "Don, never think you know what was said in the past. Even if you might be right [with me, he added, that was a long shot], revisiting past conversations does not help to resolve conflicts. It only adds to the fire."

The advice came years ago, and I'm still married.

Even when I thought I won the skirmish, I had a hunch I was losing the relationship.

That's me!

Kelly

Kelly

In a big, Chicago-area high school, I was best known as the little brother of Kelly Kuhl.

That suited me just fine. It opened up doors for me and allowed me to ask pretty girls for dates. It gave me recognition before I earned it.

Kelly is two years older than me. She has always been cool. She was a great dancer. Boys lined up at the front door of our apartment hoping for a date (popular boys). My parents named her Marlene. It didn't suit her. She named herself Kelly and it stuck with her through a remarkable career in dance and theater management.

Kelly is one of my best friends today. She has a certain spirit, courage and beauty that has lasted through the years. Whenever I need a little boost, all I need to do is give Kelly a call. It's always been that way.

I remember back in the day when she would fix the two of us a bowl of Campbell's tomato soup and a grilled cheese sandwich for lunch. They may still be the best meals I've ever enjoyed.

As I age, it's important for me to remember how lucky I've been. I had a great mom and dad. I've been blessed with loyal friends who often got me out of trouble.

And I have Kelly Kuhl as a big sister.

Walk with Me

Several major studies have indicated that meaningful friendships are the best medicine for a long, happy life. They beat out gobs of money, job success or where one might choose to live.

This got me thinking of Jerry, one of my pals in grade school. We lived about half a mile apart, with Saint Cecilia Grade School right in the middle. Without thinking a whit about it, we developed a pattern that drove our parents nuts. Many school days, Jerry would walk me home. We didn't have to say much. It just felt good to have a friend walking next to me, kicking pine cones down the sidewalk.

Approaching my house, Jerry and I would turn right around and start walking back the other way, past the school and to Jerry's house. If we were discussing something special, like toads, foods we hated the most or how to skip rocks, Jerry and I would flip around back toward Saint Cecilia. You get the picture. This could go on past dinner time.

I'd love to have a 75-year-old Jerry in my life today. Often, I've recognized what really counts is not where I'm walking to but who is walking alongside me.

Best Friends

So, I made a list of my 10 best friends.

What do they all have in common?

I came up with three personal traits:

1. All my friends are curious people. They search for answers to questions I'm only thinking about. Their curiosity leads to wisdom and unique points of view. Many people get smarter based on what they read in books or watch on television. Most of my wisdom comes from listening to my best friends.

2. All my friends speak from the heart. I never worry about getting a bunch of generic fluff. My friends have passionate sweet spots that define who they are deep inside. I may not always agree with their core beliefs, but I never question their sincerity.

3. All my friends have a sense of humor. They laugh often, especially at my expense. It's okay, because I typically earn it. And the next time, they will bear the brunt of their own joke and laugh even louder.

The antidote to loneliness is friendship.

I may be many things, but I'm rarely lonely.

So Happy to See You

I continue to learn from four of my best pals—my white Swiss shepherds.

Today's lesson: Make sure you let family and friends know how happy you are to see them. I'm not good at this yet, but I have outstanding tutors.

Nigel, Sammy, Jody Beth and Zeke have this talent down to a real science. No matter how many times a day I enter their space, they make it appear as if I'm their long-lost best buddy. Tails wag, eyes focus on my eyes—they're dog-smiling. Jody jumps up and gives my face a lick. Nigel offers me his favorite red ball. Sammy, the jokester, belts out a happy howl and Zeke maneuvers between my legs to keep me from going anywhere.

From now on, my close friends and family can count on getting my full appreciation. It won't be quite the same as my four poorly trained (thank goodness) shepherds. I'll use more human signs of love.

As we age and many of our loved ones are scattered around the globe, we never know when one particular interchange may be our last. Let's make each one stupendous.

And I promise I won't give any face licks.

My Best

Sherry and I had a little spat today. No big thing. I was being a jerk again.

Then, I failed to respond to a good friend's request. It would have been so easy to make his day.

This evening, I'm scratching my head while asking myself this question: "Do I give my very best to those I love the most?"

Often, I go out of my way to impress people I barely know. I try to create a memorable encounter. They'll walk away saying, "My, that old guy, whatever his name is, must be a wonderful fellow."

I'm writing in the front of my calendar: "Don, give your best to those who mean the most to you."

In further reflection, this is a smart, almost selfish, thing to do. Those special people in my life are the ones most apt to pay me back with spectacular moments.

Part of healthy aging is getting smarter.

"Don, give your best to those who mean the most to you."

Not Forgotten

Joey died on December 8, a cool Tuesday in 2020. I just found out today.

He lived in a small town in central Iowa. It's been over 20 years since I chatted with Joey at a little cafe on the edge of his town off Highway 30. I remember laughing until tears came to our eyes about the good old days (as if that day would not soon become another good old day).

Joey and I went to graduate school together at Iowa State. We were both getting Master of Science degrees in higher education under ISU's wonderful dean of students, Art Sandeen.

Joey had always been an excellent student. I had not. Back then, master's students had to take an oral exam before graduating. Joey was bursting with confidence. I was stammering foolishness over a beer and a hot beef sandwich. Joey urged me forward, helping me articulate the history of universities in England in the 1940s.

Later that month, I entered a bare classroom, scared to death. Three professors sat across from me. Art Sandeen smiled and gave me one of his twinkling winks. I remembered Joey's entertaining descriptions of higher education in foreign lands.

Two hours later, I left the room smiling. I knew I had nailed my oral exam.

Thanks, Joey. I will always remember.

Losing the Argument

I need help. I've been losing more than my share of arguments. I'm being bested at work, with combative friends and in the neighborhood fence wars. Looking back over my 75 years, I've prided myself on being persuasive. Others may need to use deceptive strategies to seek victory. Not me. I'm always right.

It dawns on me that I need to employ new approaches. Why not learn from the woman who wins every argument in my home? That's Sherry. I know she cheats.

For one thing, during the heat of battle, Sherry always stays as calm as if she is listening to classical music and taking a bubble bath. This in itself gets me flustered and makes my ears twitch (a beet red face and twitchy ears do not work in my favor).

Sherry also appears to pay attention to what I have to say. How fair is that in a heated argument? She never interrupts me, which is a rude but effective scheme. It forces me to actually finish a point which has not yet solidified in my own mind. I stammer a bit to gain precious seconds to compose myself. Never once does she jump in to save me. She just stands there. It's aggravating, to put it mildly.

The thing that bothers me most is Sherry uses logic to express her point of view. Arguments should stay emotional. Right? Yet she lobs fact after fact to support her position. Can you imagine how analytics throw me off my game?

The bottom line is, as I age, I've learned to copy winners. Tomorrow, when my knucklehead neighbor, Jed, argues again that my fence is on his property, I will stay calm and say, "Jed, tell me more. You have my full attention."

Collecting Friends

Many years ago, Frank Tate gave me a wonderful piece of advice that has never left me.

He said, "Don, don't trade in one friend for another. Accumulate them like rare gems. The more you have, the greater the glow."

I've been lucky. I'm blessed with many friends—a few dating back over 50 years, and others who I discovered more recently.

Each friend brings me a special gift. I bumped into Gary in first grade. We were altar boys together. My mother taught us how to bake an angel food cake when we were eight years old.

I met Larry before my freshman year in high school. We have stayed close buddies ever since. Larry knows most of the people who are important in my life. He is aware when I embellish the facts surrounding a past adventure. Yet, he says nothing. Now that's a friend.

I met Paul in college. When I travel east, we have lunch together and laugh about the untamed escapades of our youth. We agree, neither of us should have survived. We're probably right.

Then there are four more Larrys, William, Susan, two Scotts, Randy, Mike, Jake, Chris, three Jims, Adam, Billy, Judy, Mark and on and on.

Each friend provides a unique reflection of who I am deep inside. And I hope to accumulate a few new gems that glow brightly this year.

Forgiveness

Aging provides many opportunities. One is improving my ability to forgive. I've discovered that hanging onto the hurts of my past causes me nothing but pain. I looked back on a few of the biggies that have eaten up precious days of my life. It made me recognize my feelings of righteousness and victimization limited my ability to enjoy life and take in all the love around me.

I made a two-part deal several years ago. I forgave everyone I felt had unfairly hurt me in the past (I'm sure some of them were merely figments of my imagination). The second part was to seek everyone's forgiveness for my screw-ups. I knew there had been a bunch, both large and small. I made a lot of mistakes and hurt a few people I cared for greatly.

The sad part is, it was too late to make amends to those I most egregiously hurt—several are dead or lost forever. However, there is a lightness in my heart for the mere recognition that I wish to do so.

This is not a quick action. My plan for forgiveness, going both ways, has gone on for years (and still is).

Forgiveness is a pathway toward freedom and opens the gate to joyous tomorrows.

Right Turn

Why do some of my friends invest precious time with individuals who drive them nuts?

As I age, I'm getting better at only chasing after people who bring joy to my life. I hide out from those other guys who leave me on empty.

An example: I have a neighbor we'll call Marty, who wants to chat when I'm walking by. Marty knows the "secret stuff" that's going on with families who live between his house and the lake. It's always something pretty despicable. He just thinks I should have a heads-up. Since Sherry and I pride ourselves on being the most weird and private people in our neighborhood, I hate to imagine the colorful stories Marty floats about us.

For seven years, I've taken a left turn out of my driveway on my daily walk, hoping to bring a little serenity to the end of a busy day. Marty lives two houses down on the left. Often, he's waiting at his mailbox to ambush me. I can't escape. He walks with me until another terrible tale is told.

I could turn right—but then I face a huge hill that makes me sweat and breathe like a panting dog.

I just turned 75 years old. I'm smarter and wiser than when I was 74.

For my physical and mental health, I'm turning right from now on.

04

Gobble up knowledge.
There's always something you can learn.

Don, the Old Explorer

*"Man's mind stretched to a new idea never
goes back to its original dimensions."*
– Oliver Wendell Holmes, Jr.

I'm hoping the last stretch of my life continues to be one of discovery.
I wish for my mind to continue to grow, to learn new stuff about myself
and the world around me.

As I age, it takes a bit more gumption to expand into new territory. The
old and familiar appear to be safe havens. At times, I hear myself saying,
"Why should I learn about this new approach or discovery? Why don't I
close my door and stay with what feels safe and secure?"

In earlier years, I had no choice. New ideas and new gadgets exploded
all around me. I owned companies. I had kids to keep up with. I needed
to make a secure living. Now, the sense of urgency is gone. Curious and
dynamic new generations have moved into my key roles of power and
responsibility. Now, I need to take the initiative for my own sake.

My old friends can be placed in two categories: those sitting back in
rocking chairs and those continuing to be explorers.

I want to be an explorer for as long as I can.

Reading Chairs

The older I get, the more reading chairs I seize around our home. Sherry, the dominant power of the household, complains that a book or magazine of mine remains indefinitely on at least four seating areas. She attempts to gather them up and put them on a shelf, but I have taken a mighty stand.

My living room chair is blue, big and beckons me nightly. It's for my fun fiction book of the week (or sometimes month). It's currently occupied by *The Beantown Girls.* When my macho friends come over, I slide it under the cushion.

My straight back office chair has the latest copy of *The Harvard Business Review.* Occasionally, I find an article that supports my management style. I mark it all up and require our senior staff to read it.

My chair at the kitchen table is owned by the latest *New Yorker* magazine. I love the cartoons and not much else.

Finally, the chair I have claimed in the corner of our bedroom is reserved for historical biographies. Currently, Che Guevara has captured the space. I can learn a lot from Che when dealing with Sherry.

When I turn 75, I plan to go after five chairs.

Self-correction

Yesterday, I thought I observed an employee misrepresenting a situation. It was a small matter that made little difference to the overall outcome.

In earlier years, I would have challenged his statement and encouraged him to fess up.

In my senior years of managing and mentoring, I've learned to keep my trap shut.

First off, I may have it wrong. For decades, I never considered that possibility. But as my mother used to say, "the proof is in the pudding," and I've found my opinions and memories clouded by preconceived notions. More than once, when all the facts are in, I've had to apologize for correcting someone who was correct to begin with.

More importantly, most people of substance have the ability to self-correct. They don't need someone like me to point out every error of omission or colorful overstatement. Their self-talk will put them on the right track.

Besides, all of us listen better to what we tell ourselves than what others say to us. Right?

Augie the Angel

I have an oddly shaped angel who looks after me. In my daydreams, Augie appears with wings far too small for his stout body. He wears red, full-body underwear and a big white cowboy hat. Augie can't fly. It is aerodynamically impossible, but he does his best by taking long hops over the sagebrush.

Late yesterday afternoon, after an exhausting day of failing to get my points across to an assortment of friends and employees, I feel a push in my back. It's Augie, stumbling in from the west.

"Augie," I say, "Why can't you enlighten these people who don't agree with me? I thought it was an angel's job to make this earth a better place. I can't do it on my own."

Augie, half hiding under his big white cowboy hat, responds, "It's a tough job to open people up to new ways of thinking. From early childhood, you humans accumulate all kinds of beliefs that lock you into one-track thinking."

"You aren't trying hard enough, Augie," I insist. "Why don't you sneak up and scare the most cynical offender and get them to be more open-minded?"

Augie, my awkward angel, hops away and I return daydreaming about the way things should be.

Suddenly, I'm startled out of my wits.

Augie has returned, slapping one of his tiny wings in my face.

"Boo," he says to me.

P.S. I attempted to draw you a picture of Augie. I failed

Checking In

Every month I receive a financial statement on the fiscal health of The Change Companies®. The report shows our assets, liabilities, income and expenses. A few pages in, I have a pretty good idea what kind of month we had. What's great is, right next to the monthly numbers, I see where The Change Companies® was during the same time last year.

I started thinking about how helpful it would be to have a similar report on how I was doing personally each month. I could review my assets and gains, like new friends I cultivated, new adventures I uncovered, books I read and so on. On the other side of my statement, I could study my expenses. Did I fall back in some way? Did I lose a buddy? Did I shy away from helping someone in need? Did I waste an opportunity?

Just like my financial statement, my evaluation could include how I'm doing this month compared to a year ago. Am I more personally and emotionally prosperous?

Now, where can I find a personal accountant who will give me an accurate statement?

The older I get, the more curious I become about what makes me tick.

Deep Dive

Oh my goodness. What's happening to me?

Long ago, I fell in love with the work of Ira Progoff, the person who captured me with the power of intensive journaling. My curiosity could not stop. What made Ira so smart?

Ira was greatly influenced by the work of Carl Jung. This fact got me reading a book titled *Jung's Map of the Soul* by Murray Stein. Surprisingly, I liked it and understood some of it. However, it's still clear I don't understand much about what's rattling around in my brain.

What did I do next? I put a pen and paper by my bed. Every time I woke up, I started writing down immediately what I could remember about my dreams, even before using the bathroom (sometimes this is difficult for me, but that's another story). Now I'm attempting to match my dreams with Jung's soul mapping research. I'm getting totally lost in all of this but having a great time along the way.

Many of you may not wish to dive deep into your "psyche," but for those who do, I think you will find it fascinating stuff.

Bottom line: The older I get, the more curious I become about what makes me tick.

Foxtails

I'm in a great battle. My adversary is the foxtail. These weeds that look so green and engaging in the spring become a bitter enemy as they turn hay yellow and grow sharp barbs by early summer.

The only way to successfully defeat the foxtail is to grab it firmly at the base and pull out the entire root. If you mow or just pull out the tassels, the foxtail returns with a vengeance and the problem escalates over time.

So yesterday I'm on my hands and knees pulling out hundreds of these weeds that have invaded our property.

It's not exciting work, so my mind wanders to my past. Early in my life, I had my own form of foxtails. I was not robustly honest in dealing with people who loved me. I used alcohol to hide my fears. I blamed others for my "bad luck."

When I got pricked by the barbs of my foxtails, I would just yank at the tops rather than get at the roots of my negative behavior. My foxtails just grew stronger.

Over time, smart people explained I needed to pull out the entire root.

I did.

Thank goodness.

I'll Wow You When I'm Really, Really Old

When I get really, really old, I'm going to be smarter and better organized. I've already made my list:

I will know where my wallet, phone and keys are at all times.

I will transfer my list of contacts from my notepad to my cellphone.

I will know how to use Uber rather than just pretending I do.

I will study the basic research behind why doughnuts and ice cream are bad for me.

I will find my little white box of dental floss.

I will change the oil in my car before the red light goes on.

I will match my socks as soon as they come out of the dryer.

I will not be caught wearing one dark blue and one black sock (refer to above).

I already know that Easter is on a Sunday. In addition, I will learn why it is on a particular Sunday.

I will put this list in a safe and secure place. I will remember where that place is.

Thank goodness I don't have to start this until I'm really, really old.

Being Mindful of My Meditation

My efforts at meditation aren't going so well. I recently read about the benefits of meditation—particularly for people my age—but I don't seem to be mindful enough while attempting to meditate.

First off, I thought meditation and mindfulness were kind of the same thing. Boy, was I wrong. The experts let me know that being mindful is showing up at the thing I'm doing. Like brushing my teeth. I should smell the spearmint of my toothpaste and appreciate the sounds of my brush swishing around my implants. While I'm brushing my teeth, if I'm thinking about whether I remembered to mail in my income tax, I'm not being mindful—and missing out on all the potential benefits.

Meditation is a more structured practice. I'm trying to do it for an hour each week with a group of my older friends. We find a comfortable place to sit. We close our eyes. Then we focus on our breathing. In... and out... in... and out. A leader reads a passage meant to bring loving-kindness and inner peace.

My mind strays. I start thinking about whether I did a good job brushing my teeth. And then there's that income tax thing.

How Lucky Was I?

Still in my 20s, I had the opportunity to spend time with Carl Rogers. I was working at a small, experimental college at Lake Tahoe in the 1970s. Rogers and his wife, Helen, visited on several weekends and shared his vision about life.

Back in the 1940s, Rogers had developed person-centered therapy, an approach that influenced the way therapists worked with clients for decades that followed. At our small college, he helped students and faculty members recognize that every human being strives for and has the capacity to fulfill his or her own potential.

This kind, brilliant man helped change the way I looked at my own life. Rather than searching for someone to tell me what I should or should not do, Rogers encouraged me to look within myself for the right answers.

Fifty years later, I sit on my back porch paging through books written by experts who are telling me how to sketch out my remaining years. A lot of fine research has gone into their recommendations.

As I doze off, I see Carl Rogers putting his hand on my shoulder and saying softly, "Don, look inside. Listen to the one who knows you best."

By golly, I think that's me.

Curiosity

If I could pass one piece of advice to the younger me, it would be to practice being more interested than interesting.

For decades I attempted to be an interesting guy to both friends and acquaintances. I had jokes and stories relevant to any group. Didn't people want to learn where I had been and what I had done? Often, I embellished the truth.

To my surprise, I didn't attract a crowd, often not a single person.

Around my mid-30s, I began to have a legitimate interest in what others had to say more than my own blathering.

By my 50s, I searched for people smarter than me, which was an easy quest. They had wondrous things to share.

Now, in my 70s, I'm blessed with an insatiable curiosity with many friends to tap. This aging stuff has its advantages.

Well-read

What's wrong with me? Attempting to pick up little nuggets that will serve me in my elder years, I've purchased yet another self-help book. I have so many hardbound guidebooks to serenity, I can set them up like dominoes. Just a nudge, and one book will fall on the next one and then the next and so on. If I'm careful and use my hardwood floor, I'm capable of putting on quite a show. As they tumble along, I will have the cascading books spell out the word HELP in cursive.

My latest book is on resilience. Among other tips, it's teaching me to reframe my negative thoughts.

For example, when I was leaving the Costco parking lot yesterday, this knucklehead pulled right out in my lane. I swerved off the road to avert a crash. The inattentive driver, in his black BMW, blared his horn while gesturing with a finger to show me he was number one.

According to my new book, my negative thoughts needed immediate reframing.

I totally failed to use my mental resilience strategies for reframing. I stayed in my "catch up with this jerk" mode.

I think I need to purchase another self-help book.

05

Accept what is.

Have gratitude for where you are.

The Circle of Life in the Denver Airport

At Denver International Airport I spotted a baby looking around as if he lost something important. He quietly burped and may have released a short burst of gas. It made his whole face smile, as if he had pulled a fast one on unsuspecting travelers. The baby stared across at the Cinnabon store. I could tell he was interested in sweet exploration, but his legs were not up to independent travel. He settled back and softly closed his eyes. The baby looked content and satisfied. I guessed he was imagining all the adventures he had in store.

At Denver International Airport I spotted an old man looking around as if he had lost something important. He quietly burped and may have released a short burst of gas. It made his whole face smile, as if he had pulled a fast one on unsuspecting travelers. The old man stared across at the Cinnabon store. I could tell he was interested in sweet exploration, but his legs were not up to independent travel. He settled back and softly closed his eyes. The old man looked content and satisfied. I guessed he was remembering all the adventures he had experienced.

Top of My Game

With my lower back issues, it's getting increasingly difficult for me to walk upstairs.

That didn't keep me from a Wisconsin Badger Football game last weekend. Right before halftime, I began the climb from my row up to the second level of Camp Randall Stadium. The first 15 or 20 steps were okay but then the pain and lack of mobility kicked in. I bore down like any great fan would. I stared at each step, gritted my teeth and used my right arm and hand to drive my right leg up and forward.

The band was playing the Wisconsin fight song. Cheers were coming from the 80,000 in attendance. I kept plowing up the cement steps looking for daylight.

At the top a small group of ladies dressed in Bucky Badger garb gave me an empathetic cheer in unison, "We were hoping you could make it to the top!"

For a brief moment I felt embarrassment for making an awkward scene.

Then I smiled and gave them each a high five.

"Sweetie"

One little thing that bugs me is when I'm in a coffee shop and a young, often attractive, waitress calls me "honey" or "sweetie."

I don't translate those words to anything other than "old man." A guy in his 30s or 40s sits down in the stool next to me and the same waitress doesn't call him "sweetie." And I'll bet he's a sweeter guy at the moment than me because he's not stewing over what a nice young woman trying to make a living just called him.

I know I'm overly sensitive about this. In former days, I might take such greetings from a waitress as a compliment, thinking, *Wow, I must look particularly handsome today.*

As I'm keystroking this blog, I just caught a reflection of my face on my computer screen. Now, I'm rethinking my whole mindset about such greetings. If anyone looks at my unshaved, thin-haired, bifocaled, sagging-jowled face and calls me "sweetie," there is only one appropriate response.

"Thank you."

Gridlocks in Life

During certain years of my life, I spent many hours in traffic gridlocks in major cities like Boston, Seattle, Chicago and Dallas. My impatience and frustration reached great heights.

Washington, D.C. drove me nuts. One summer rush hour (actually many hours), it dawned on me to pull over at the first available exit. I cruised into a Dairy Queen and had a chocolate milkshake while I watched the cars on the freeway inch along. The break was therapeutic, and I still reached my destination.

It took me another 30 years to catch on that this was one way of handling major disagreements I had with friends and colleagues. Often, due to stubbornness or hurt feelings, such disagreements reached a gridlock. We'd inch along, losing our cool and allowing other pleasures to be lost along the way.

Now, in my 70s and still disliking gridlocks, I ask myself each time I reach an impasse with a close friend, Is this the time for me to pull over for a break and have a chocolate milkshake?

Often, the gridlock clears before my final slurp.

Ugly Motels and Magical Kingdoms

Hey, Don Kuhl. You've been screwing up. At your age, it's high time to accept your frequent blunders and make the most out of the consequences.

Great example: I was recently in Orlando, Florida, for a conference, staying in the ugliest motel of all-time because the host hotel was fully booked weeks earlier. My room had a lumpy bed and one chair that survived the 1970s. The soiled curtains did not cover the width of the dirty windows looking out on a swimming pool that was closed for repairs. The yellow walls had no artwork other than a weird poster of a golf ball floating in tomato juice. My next-door neighbors were cheering on some soccer game. Overhearing their conversation, it sounded like they were running out of beer. It was 10 in the morning.

So obviously, Don, you made a poor choice in selecting a motel.

My mood became one of self-loathing. I could have booked a room earlier at the Hilton across the road. Why did I wait so long? My next thought went to my friends and colleagues who undoubtedly were enjoying the luxurious amenities at the beautiful Hilton: warm cookies upon arrival, large walk-in showers and plenty of plush white towels.

The new me, however, recognized these facts: I saved nearly $100, I had the opportunity to walk each sunny day to and from the conference and I met a great couple from Michigan whose three children were having the time of their lives while wearing Mickey Mouse ears.

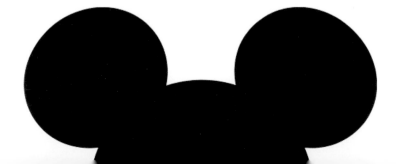

Ahead of the Curve

Here I am, staring at my third week of recovery from my total hip replacement. I joined nearly 2.5 million people in the United States who are walking around with artificial hips. In the next 12 months, another 300,000 individuals will join our club.

I'm not very good at recovering from anything. I don't like it. I have this irrational opinion I should be way in front of average timelines for returning to normal states of activity. My body does not agree with me and lets me know by providing sharp reality checks when I step out of line.

Driving my car was a great example. After the first week, I thought I should be able to navigate through Carson City. I didn't want to run over any pedestrians I like, so I decided to practice going around my driveway, starting and stopping. My neighbor, Dave, who always has thought I'm a little bit nuts, happened to see my circular route and quickly called my wife to report my strange behavior.

Thanks, neighbor Dave. My wife hid my car keys for another week, perhaps saving the lives of fellow Nevadans while reminding me to focus on walking in a straight line.

Dawn

Well into my 70s, I wish I could say I've become a patient guy. But little things still bother me, and I can get in a bad mood over the smallest matters.

However, I've discovered the perfect spot to practice being a better person. It's my local Starbucks. Throngs of coffee lovers enter Starbucks and seem to fall under a magical spell of compliance and joy. Except me.

I enter and find customers beaming, waiting in line to describe in detail the exact syrups and toppings to add to their grande coffees. I watch an unnaturally happy barista printing precise instructions on each cup, including the first name of the customer. The cups get passed to jubilant employees who grind, whip and concoct each order, while the smiling customers wait patiently for their names to be called.

It's my turn. I order a small, black coffee, extra hot. I speak out confidently, "My name is Don." With a big smile on my face, I retreat and wait for my name to be announced. I try to project patience as I hear other names called out merrily: Eric, Marissa, Tammy, Megan, Patrick.

I make a promise to myself. Whenever my name is finally called, I will sashay forward, graciously accept the cup that says "Dawn," and when I'm told to have an "extra fun day," that's exactly what I will have.

Handsome Dad

When my dad, Vern, was about the age I am today, he moved in with us. He had been known to be a handsome man, but I didn't think he looked too hot anymore.

For one thing, his hair had thinned, and it was a drab shade of gray.

He wore shorts when he walked our property. He had lost all of the hair on his legs. Much worse, he wore those thin, white compression socks that hugged his skinny ankles. His doctor said it kept him from getting blood clots. I thought they made him look ridiculous.

My dad also walked with a noticeable limp, often with a pained look on his white face.

Today, I looked at a picture of Vern back at that time.

I look a lot like him now. My hair is thin and gray. I walk with a limp. Last week, my doctor gave me a pair of white compression socks.

I've changed my mind.

My dad was a darn good-looking man every day of his life.

Vern at 3 years old

Climb the Mountain

It isn't how far or how fast I go up the mountain. It's whether I get started.

I'm blessed with living on the side of a mountain. Twenty years ago I could go out my back door and hike the 22 miles up to Lake Tahoe.

Five years ago I made it to a bubbling creek about half way to the lake.

Last weekend, I climbed around 300 yards above my house. It took more effort than my 22-mile hike two decades ago. And on that sunny Sunday, I looked back and saw the beauty of the land, the beauty of the decades.

You know what? Next year, I'm still going to go out that same back door, and I'll appreciate the view no matter how far up I get.

It isn't how far or how fast I go up the mountain. It's whether I get started.

Negotiating Last Place

A few years ago, I went to a three-day workshop on the strategies of negotiation. On the first day, I was told that in life and in business, you receive not what you deserve, but what you negotiate.

After learning some ways of being crafty, almost deceptive, the class split up in pairs and were given business scenarios. Our acumen was filmed to be evaluated and judged by the instructor and fellow students.

I couldn't get it out of my darn head that I wanted to be more fair than clever. Why not have both sides do well?

There were sixteen in our class of high-charging business leaders. I was the eldest by at least a decade. In the final hour of the workshop, we each received our class rank. I came in sixteenth.

Flying home, I was kind of proud of myself.

Jeff at 4 years old

Remembering 50

It's so weird. My son turned 50. How can that be? I was 50 just a few years ago. Wasn't I?

If you have children and you remember "The Howdy Doody Show," there's a good chance your children no longer consider themselves young—or you as anything but old. Not that they will say anything about your stage in life. They're too worried about their own.

It got me thinking. Would I rather be 50 or in my mid-70s?

I think back to where I was at 50. I felt I was always late to something. Often, I was. My basketball jump shot had changed to a push shot (my son claims it always was a push shot). I received my first temporary membership card from the AARP. When a tire went flat, I couldn't remember where the auto company hid my jack. All my financial attention was focused on my checking account. I had no savings account. I still thought young ladies would smile at me when we passed in the shopping mall. They did not.

I compare all that to my status today. It's rare when I know I'm late to anything. I can still sink 7 out of 10 from the free-throw line. I don't even pretend to think about changing one of my tires. Now, young ladies smile and open the door for me.

I'm happy I still remember Buffalo Bob.

Inside Out

I was having coffee with a close friend, Mike, talking about getting older together. We looked around the shop and guessed the ages of people standing in line. Were they younger or older than us? It took an evaluation of at least a dozen customers before we found one who might have been born before 1945, our magic year.

Mike said, "My body has changed so much over the last few years, but I feel like I'm exactly the same guy inside I've always been."

I don't consider Mike brilliant, or even particularly gifted, but I thought his statement was profound.

There are two Dons, the outside me and the inside me.

People who don't know me judge who I am by the outside Don.

Close friends can joke with me about what the outside Don is becoming, but they have a love and appreciation for the inside Don.

The big question is, do I care too much about the outside me? Occasionally, when I meet an acquaintance I have not seen for several years, I think they are saying to themselves, "What in the hell happened to Don?" In reality, they are probably just trying to think of my name.

No, the real Don is the inside me. I like what Mike said. He is the same wonderful guy I've known for 20 years. In fact, for all of us, the good stuff is housed on our insides.

An Earful

I'm sure people told me I needed hearing aids long before now. I just couldn't hear them. And I wasn't thrilled about sticking little wires in my ears.

Last week, I sneaked into a hearing aid specialty store just to look around.

An hour later, I wore fancy hearing aids. For a short time, I was aware of sounds I had forgotten existed. Did you know when you rub your hands together, it creates a wispy noise? Not only that, but shoes make a clicking sound on linoleum. Wow!

My superpower was short-lived.

First off, you must know I have big, weird-looking ears. One sticks out a bit from my head. Like I'm a half Dumbo.

Second, I lose track of what I should be paying attention to. It's called aging.

So, the techie part of my aids is supposed to lie securely on top of each of my strange ears.

My right hearing aid was dislodged and fell into the toilet bowl before I left the hearing aid store. I squeamishly fished it out, washed it in the sink and stuck it back on my ear.

That should have been a sign. Two hours later, I reached up to feel my new equipment, and they were both gone.

Maybe it was taking off my mask (attached to my unique ears). Maybe it was putting on my sunglasses. It could have been my tussle with the dogs going up the mountain.

My expensive hearing aids are somewhere in the state of Nevada. I don't know where.

You can laugh at me now. I won't hear you.

Gabby

I have an old friend who is making daily visits now. After two back surgeries and two new hips, Gabby, my chronic pain pal, is waking me up each morning and sometimes following me to work.

Back in an earlier day, chronic pain controlled much of my life. I'd try to hide from it or pretend it wasn't there. I'd get depressed or anxious just thinking about all my pain. I felt sorry for myself.

Then Steve Hayes, a friend and gifted researcher, shared his work called Acceptance and Commitment Therapy (ACT). I didn't understand everything Steve was talking about, but I think he advised me to quit hiding out from my pain and incorporate it into my daily life.

I called my pain Gabby. I took him for walks. I told him he wasn't as tough as he claimed to be. I even made fun of Gabby when no one was watching. My life got better, even with Gabby tagging along.

Then, thanks to some gifted surgeons, Gabby took off for a while.

Gabby must have missed me, because he's returned.

However, this time I'm ready for him. Just last night, I told Gabby he can never take a front row seat. He's lost his clout as far as I'm concerned.

Still So Young

Sometimes I feel so young I need to do a search of my body to prove I'm approaching 75 years of age.

My search doesn't take a long time.

Typically, I first look down at my hands. They are a palm reader's dream come true—so many deep canyons to explore. My fingers look like little dessert bars that were forgotten in a cabinet years ago. I flip to the back of my hands to discover these blue veins that pop up when I make a fist. If I squint just right, the knuckle of my middle finger resembles the face of the old cartoon character Mr. Magoo.

My search goes from my hands to my feet. I don't expect much, because my feet have never been a game changer for me. That's why I always wear socks. My little toes have never touched the ground, but now I think they wish to express themselves by climbing on top of the next toe. They look like bunk beds for tiny pink piglets.

I'll spare you and stop reporting on my search.

The weird thing is, after all that visual evidence, my silly head keeps telling me I'm still so young.

Augie to the Rescue

Augie, my clumsy angel, was giving me another one of his lectures.

He caught me "saying bad words" as I attempted to button my shirt—a real chore due to my severe carpal tunnel syndrome.

Augie: "I taught you better than this. My Boss created pullover shirts that have no buttons."

Me: "You aren't exactly a fashion statement with your stubby wings. Why don't you shut up while I mindfully finish dressing? I still have my shoe-tying challenge ahead."

Augie: "You poor unimaginative soul. Even dapper Saint Peter switched to loafers decades ago."

Me, more perturbed: "Why did you stumble into my bedroom anyway?"

Augie, departing: "I wanted to be certain you had the gift I gave you 30 years ago still hanging above your bed."

I looked up on my wall and saw my framed, faded copy of The Serenity Prayer.

P.S. I'm still trying to draw Augie. No luck.

Hands of Silk

As I age, my hands are getting softer.

That's a real problem because they've never been muscular or tough to the touch. So many people over the years, after I've attempted to give a firm, cowboy-like handshake, remark, "My, your hands are really soft."

I don't take it as a compliment. After all, I'm from Carson City, where men before me helped tame the Wild West. The hands of real men lassoed stallions, put up barbed wire fences and dug for gold and silver with picks and shovels.

My hands feel as if they've soaked in Jergens lotion for a week. They have kind of a soft pink glow.

It isn't that I haven't tried to build calluses. I pull weeds without my gloves on. I scoop up boulders bigger than basketballs and heave them into my pickup truck. I rub sand back and forth in my bare palms when no one is looking.

I'll bet you think I'm too sensitive about something that's not a big deal. You might be right, but let's not shake on it.

A Sticking Point

Manufacturers of cups, plates, tables and picture frames have been tracking my aging process. They hate me. Yet, they want my money.

For all my previous years, we have gotten along well. They make stuff. I buy their stuff. It's been a symbiotic relationship. Then, they turned on me—just about the time I turned 65.

Nine years ago, in a secret meeting room in a suburb of Chicago, they got together to plot against me.

Plate maker: "Let's use our magic glue on price stickers and put them on the bottom of anything Don purchases."

Picture frame maker: "I'll stick my label right on the glass. I'll turn up one corner so it will look like a no-brainer for Don to pull off."

Table maker: "Hee, hee, hee. He's getting old. He has those dull scissors he uses to scratch off labels. I bet he cuts himself on his wrinkled pinky finger."

Cup maker: "Super. With his daily aspirin, Don will bleed on his new rug."

Plate maker: "And the old guy has no idea where he put his box of Band-Aids."

So, for nearly 10 years now, my house has been full of products with little white label leftovers securely attached.

I pretend not to notice them. And my Band-Aids stay in the top left drawer.

In My Own Skin

As long as I can remember, I've had this nagging fear of being around people. I stuttered as a kid—a friend told me last week I still do—and always felt like I was letting someone down, although I wasn't sure who exactly. I tried to mask my fear. Years ago, I drank alcohol in excess to feel comfortable in my own skin. That was a big mistake.

Then there was a period of time that I worked extra hard at having everyone like me. I thought the fear might go away. It didn't, and I'm certain not everyone liked me. A few people told me as much.

One great thing about getting older is that I don't have that nagging, vague fear nearly as much. I've learned to stick around folks I enjoy and excuse myself from those who make me feel uncomfortable. I've learned to be comfortable in my own skin.

One more thing. I know a few people really, really love me. Ahh, that feels stupendous.

Do you get confused between chores you have to do and chores you get to do? I do.

Petunia Patrol

Do you get confused between chores you have to do and chores you get to do? I do.

An example: I've been charged with watering our 16 flower pots, which hang from trees and balconies around our house. During the heat of summer, it's almost a daily job and takes nearly an hour.

I love the beauty of the flowers, even though I don't know the names of most of them—and those I do, I can't pronounce. I've chosen to call them all petunias.

On days I'm in a funky mood, watering feels like a chore I need to do. I figure I could be reading a book or watching the news or chatting with a friend, rather than dragging this green hose from one side of the house to the other.

When I'm in a happy mood, I talk to all my petunias. I watch my dogs sit under the pots to receive cool drips of water from above. I see dozens of butterflies flutter about and watch six hawks float effortlessly in the sky.

As I age, it's wise for me to recognize I'm in control of my state of mind.

It's a real treat, watering all these petunias.

It's a Dream

I've never been a sound sleeper. For many years, I figured most bright people stayed awake thinking about stuff that had just happened or things that may be coming their way tomorrow. What a shock to learn that hours of continuous, deep sleep are actually considered healthy. Sleep is what makes the best folks tick.

I still don't get it. Why waste time dozing when much reflection and anticipation can be realized between the hours of 11 p.m. and 6 a.m.?

A friend bet me that I was sleeping just fine and dreaming about not going to sleep. That made me pay special attention to the clock on the table near my bed. That way, I could monitor my actual hours of non-sleep. No friend was going to cheat me out of my talent for not being able to comfortably doze at night.

My doctor told me I was getting a little loco about the whole deal. He said sleep is a major contributor to good health and vitality, especially for older folks like me. He told me I can call him at any time to discuss this important issue.

I plan to call him this evening around midnight. I'll lead off by imitating the voice of my favorite cartoon character, Bugs Bunny, and say, "Hey, what's up, Doc?"

Gold Medal

I'm an Olympian competing in a newly sanctioned sport: aging well.

My secret is refiguring the scoring methodology.

Actually, until I took charge, I wasn't doing so hot. My doctor held up the number 6 (based on my darn blood pressure readings). My accountant dropped me to a 4 (late tax return in 2020). My best friend gave me 7.5 (a bit disappointing after all I've done for him). My wife... oh, let's forget about that score. In contrast, the Chinese competitor averaged an 8, the Australian octogenarian received an 8.5 and the upstart old man from Namibia led the field with a 9.

I rushed over to the scoring table and shredded all the judges' signs.

When it comes to an aging competition, I believe the only number that really counts is the one you give yourself. I've given myself a perfect 10.

Now, can someone help me find the winner's podium?

06

Me and Gary making cupcakes for charity (and six for us)

Be kind.

It's always the wisest choice.

Acts of Kindness

As a youth, the word *kindness* bugged me. It sounded grandmotherly, even a bit unmasculine. I'd rather people think of me as showing toughness or courageousness. And, if someone bestowed kindness on me, I'd think I must be weak or needy.

Last week, while in line at a convenience store, I saw an elderly man fumbling in his wallet for the dollars necessary to pay for a couple items. He came up a few dollars short even after pulling change out of both front pockets. After some embarrassing moments, the man chose a box of Corn Chex to return to the cereal aisle. Just then, a long-haired kid holding two six packs of Bud Lite reached down and scooped a five-dollar bill off the floor. He told the man he saw it fall out of his wallet. The man's transaction was completed with no further fuss.

I watched this kid return one of his six packs to the beer cooler.

Now, after a lifetime of experience, the quality of kindness tops my list of favorite attributes.

Ms. Keefe

Back in high school, I had this old, old journalism teacher by the name of Ms. Keefe. She was brutal when it came to curbing my creative writing talents. I had a weekly column in a Chicago suburban newspaper that she had set up for me. I was to write interesting stories about what was happening around Lyons Township High School, and she needed to approve them before they were submitted.

Ms. Keefe was so picky. She chopped my outstanding flowing copy into short sentences. She made me drop most of my adjectives and adverbs. Sometimes she edited out entire paragraphs. Ms. Keefe made me write my first sentences over and over again.

Even with her whittling down my unique style, several of my features got picked up by the *Chicago Tribune,* which was a pretty cool thing for a high school kid.

My grade point average sucked when I attempted to enroll at the University of Illinois.

I found out Ms. Keefe secretly sent a letter of recommendation on my behalf. Somehow, I got in. I never thanked her.

Fifty years later I looked at my old high school yearbook. There was a picture of Kay Keefe, not a year over 45.

Lyons Township High School, LaGrange, Ill.

That's Lyons Township High School,
North Campus

Jacob

As a young guy, I had an opportunity to run a full-service hotel on West Colfax in Denver. The Four Winds was owned by an 80-year-old Jewish businessman by the name of Jacob. He liked to hang out at the hotel and bother me. What a waste of time for me to babysit this ancient character while managing the hotel, restaurant and bar.

I was stuck looking after Jacob early each morning while he cleaned the coffee urn with great thoroughness, so guests could enjoy a fresh cup of coffee. I watched him inspect the dry-aging quarters of beef in the cooler and set the thermometer to the perfect level. I tagged along while Jacob greeted each family checking in at the front desk and then followed him to the lounge where he polished the crystal wine glasses. One time I caught Jacob slipping a 20-dollar bill to our mentally impaired dishwasher, but I said nothing.

Over the years, my career progressed to manage larger hotels, but for some strange reason, I always remembered Jacob.

The Rescuer

One of my favorite paintings is The Rescuer by MacKenzie Thorpe. It hangs in our dining room and portrays a shepherd carrying a white sheep on his back through steep grass before a storm hits.

It makes me think of how all of us in days gone by have been the rescued sheep in times of personal challenge and, at other times, played the part of the shepherd providing safety to someone in need.

I think it's one of the true beauties of humanity. Our shepherds may have been parents or teachers or even strangers. At vulnerable moments they saw a storm approaching in our lives and they carried us to safety.

I figure as I age, there are more opportunities to be a shepherd and repay the countless kindnesses that strong and sensitive individuals have bestowed on me over my many years. Those moments can come at any time, at anyplace.

I just need to be ready.

Good Old Joe

I know an old guy by the name of Joe. I'm guessing he's about my age. Joe's done some amazing things the right way. He married his high school sweetheart and raised four children. He had one job his whole life and retired with high corporate honors. He lives in a brown house with a white picket fence about a mile from me.

Joe is publicly proud and secretly lonely. His wife, Emily, died two years ago. His kids have their own kids and careers. The closest lives 500 miles away. Joe has a rocking chair on his front porch. In sun, rain or snow, he rocks and rocks and ruminates about days gone by.

Friends and neighbors fondly remember Joe as a man of influence and kindness. They drive by and wave at Joe. Joe waves back and rocks—rocks in his loneliness and isolation.

We all know a Joe. Be late for the meeting or dinner. Pull in the driveway and give Joe a hug. He deserves it. So do you.

Hopper Copper

When I was a kid in a small town, our streets were patrolled by a policeman, Officer Hogan.

We neighborhood boys called him Hopper Copper because he walked with a limp from a World War II injury. We liked to keep him busy by playing little pranks. We'd swipe Christmas lights from one neighbor's yard and decorate the house across the street. We'd toilet-paper the houses of girls in our seventh-grade class and put strawberry jelly in their mailboxes.

When we played basketball under the lights at Brookfield Park, it cost us a dime an hour to keep the lights on. We pretended we were playing to a huge crowd, but our only fan was Officer Hogan. When our hour was up, the lights would make a soft pop and fade slowly. Hopper Copper always had an extra dime in his pocket to light up our courts and our lives.

Sometimes we crossed the line and did something that could get us in real trouble. Hopper Copper knew where we lived and stopped to see our parents. He always started out by saying we were "good kids, but..." Our dads provided the corporal punishment (common in those days) and made us apologize to Officer Hogan. In those cases, Hopper Copper always looked me in my 12-year-old eyes, gave me a firm handshake and told me I was a good young man.

I never did thank Hopper Copper for all the caregiving he provided to my friends and me. I wish I could do it today.

Pass the Grey Poupon

My mom played a cool trick on me when I was a little boy. She would pretend she couldn't get a jar of peanut butter open and then ask me to give it a shot. To my joyous surprise, I was able to get the lid off every time.

I took this special talent into adulthood, opening jars of pickles, olives, jellies and any other sealed packaging that others found challenging.

Recently, however, manufacturers have been messing with me. They have put their lids on more tightly than ever. I'm struggling, and I don't like it one bit.

A few weeks ago, I was losing a tussle with a jar of Grey Poupon mustard. My grandson asked if he could try to get the lid off. He gave it a couple tugs and passed the unopened jar back to me, saying, "Sorry, Grandpa. I can't open it either. Maybe you should give it one last shot."

I smiled as I opened the mustard bottle with ease.

As I age, I notice so many of the little kindnesses in life come full circle.

As I age, I notice so many of the little kindnesses in life come full circle.

Older and Kinder

Join me in this exploration. Choose three people in your life today who you respect the most.

I've got my three. One is a woman in her 30s. The second and third are old friends in their senior years.

The one connecting point is that each individual has consistently demonstrated the virtue of kindness. It's the first card they always draw from their deck of possible behaviors.

I wish I could say I show kindness on a daily basis, but I can't. So much gets in my way. Often I'm too quick to evaluate a person, as if I know what motivates them to act in a certain way. Or I get too caught up in what's in my best interest. Often, I just don't think about how a simple act of kindness could change the moment and bring relief to another human being.

Many years ago, I fired an employee on the spot for screaming at me and calling me a jerk in front of the whole staff. Months later, I found out his wife had been in a serious accident the night before. He was three hours late for work, missed a meeting with a major client, and I jumped all over him for his incompetence.

The three people I respect the most would have handled the situation in a wiser, kinder fashion. A lack of knowledge is not an excuse. Kindness beats out anger, indifference and self-righteousness every time.

I'm getting older.

And kinder.

I hope.

What Counts

Jody Beth, my faithful pup, brings me my cane I left in the bird garden. The carved, wooden handle of my cane is dangling, chewed up. The cane is useless.

As told to me by my mother a hundred times, when her mother was dying upstairs, little Donnie Kuhl, age three or so, mixed up a glass of Kool-Aid to take upstairs for his grandma.

By the time little Donnie mastered the final stair, no Kool-Aid was left in the glass. Grandma's thirst went unquenched. My ailing grandma reached out and gave me a big hug anyway. My mom did, too.

Today, I put the cane in the trash barrel and got on my knees to give Jody Beth a big hug.

For 70 years now, I have witnessed many gestures of kindness. Whether the handle has been mangled or the glass shows up empty doesn't matter much in the big scheme of life. It's the gesture that counts.

Darn Lucky

I was so darn lucky.

As a kid, I'd go to the Five and Dime, sit on a red bar stool and order a chocolate malt. Next to my huge malt glass, this beautiful waitress would sneak me the "extra" in a shiny tin container.

I was so darn lucky.

I'd go to Grandma Kuhl's house for Sunday dinner and join the "little kids" at a card table next to where the adults dined. Us kids would be dressed to the nines from church but, when my dad gave the nod, we'd fly out the back door to play tag in the alley.

I was so darn lucky.

Some girls in high school thought I was cute and kind of funny. I'd steal a kiss on the second date. Sometimes.

I was so darn lucky.

After an unimpressive college career (to put it kindly), Iowa State University gave me an opportunity to earn a Master of Science degree and discover that knowledge, after all, was a good thing.

I was so darn lucky.

After failing a few times in business, I hit a hot streak the last 40 years or so and did just fine.

Not everyone was as darn lucky as me.

Now is the time to share my luck. I wish to give everyone who is struggling the "extra" in a shiny tin container.

A Fawn

Last Saturday, Sherry and I found a dead doe on our property who had recently given birth. We sadly disposed of the body, which showed no signs of disease or wounds.

The next morning, our four white Swiss shepherds surrounded a tiny fawn and guided her gently down the mountain and toward our front porch. I've never seen anything like it. Each time the little deer attempted to slip away on wobbly legs, our dogs shepherded her closer to our doorway.

Sherry grabbed a couple blankets and wrapped the baby fawn in her lap while Nigel, Sammy, Jody Beth and Zeke sat proudly by.

My friend Larry got on the phone to find a place to take our new pal on a Sunday morning. After hours of searching, Larry found a friendly voice at Safe Haven Wildlife Sanctuary, located east of Lovelock, Nevada—over 150 miles from Washoe Valley. We took off in a windstorm with our baby fawn in the back of my Chevy Suburban.

We arrived at a magical place. Three grad students were waiting to comfort the fawn and get her to drink goat's milk from a bottle. The owner, Lynda Sugasa, took us for a tour of the sanctuary, where lions, tigers, bears and any other abandoned and injured wild animal can live in safety and peace.

That darn fawn ate up my whole day. And it was the best Sunday I've spent in a blue moon.

If life is compared to a thriving business, love is the currency that makes it successful.

Lucky in Love

I'm a lucky guy. I receive love from quite a large number of people. It comes in many forms, from close intimacy with a few individuals to acts of kindness and recognition from many others. Love drives me upward when I'm at my best. It also gives me footholds when I need to climb out of a hole I've fallen into.

Part of my luck is by design, based on the love that flows out from me. I see that love is similar to the concentric circles created when a rock is thrown into a pond. I'm the rock, and I must love myself in order for the waves of endearment to move outward. The closest circle is formed by those who make up my inner life: my wife, children and grandchildren. The second ripple is made up of my close friends and colleagues. Outer ripples come from acquaintances within the community, clients our companies have served over many years and thousands of friends from blogs I have written over the years.

In my opinion, if one's life is compared to a thriving business, love is the currency that makes it successful.

07

Celebrating my birthday!

Celebrate small pleasures.

Everyday joys can last a lifetime.

Little Joys

Maybe I'm not like most people, but seeking out the little joys of each day did not cross my mind until I was well into my 50s. Too much buzz was taking place before then.

Much of my early years can best be described as being in survival mode—just hanging on to whatever my hands could grasp.

When it wasn't a matter of survival, I was busy searching out what might give me a quick jolt of pleasure, like those little bottles filled with caffeine you see in convenience stores nowadays.

Seeking out joyous moments in my life today is a different pursuit. Often it begins with me just being still. Hearing my breathing. Counting my steps on the sidewalk. Petting my dog's belly. Eating a piece of cinnamon toast like my mother used to make. Reading a page from Tom Sawyer again. Following an ant down the side of my pine tree. Bouncing a basketball in the driveway. Hearing a train whistle from beyond the hill. Putting on the watch my father gave me. Opening the door for a man at the grocery store.

Such joyous moments rarely take place in front of my television set or computer screen.

Blue Dog

As I get older I'm finding what I put on my walls counts a whole bunch. After all, I go by the same walls 10 or 20 times in a day. I love to stare at pieces created by talented artists that speak to me. And I often speak back.

I have a blue dog riding in a convertible with his ears flopping madly in the wind. He tells me not to be so uptight all the time. I tell him that real dogs aren't blue.

What's on your walls?

Painting by Michelle Mardis

Staying a Kid

This is really cool.

As I get older, I'm discovering my opportunity to return to things that made me giggle with delight when I was a little kid. And I don't care what the neighbors say. This is one of the wonderful freedoms of aging into our 70s, 80s and beyond.

I'm becoming an expert on this, so heed a few recommendations:

Give a name to everything you care about: your favorite tree, a big boulder in the park, your stuffed animal (I know you have one). Then, speak to it by name each time you cross its path. It may take a month or so, but soon you will get whispered responses from them, full of wisdom and delight.

Be like my friend Hugh, who wrote me just today: "And now I have to head out to start crafting my annual snow mountain for the kids... and myself."

Play more games: card games, board games and any game featuring a ball. You may wish to stay away from games you played in your explorative teens.

Make your best dance moves in front of a full-length mirror and then hold up a sign with a big number 10.

I'm still working on the last one. And the problem isn't in making the sign.

Classical Greenhouse

I'm spoiled. I admit it.

One pleasure I have in the middle of winter is a tiny greenhouse in my backyard. It's not much for growing flowers or vegetables, but it feels so good to be me when I'm sitting in my broken chair, sipping hot chocolate with marshmallows and listening to the Franz Liszt Chamber Orchestra playing Mozart (it features this fabulous French horn).

Here's the deal. It's cold outside and it's snowing like crazy. My greenhouse has a tiny heater that keeps the temperature around 50 degrees—just perfect. The door is open a crack so my four shepherds can come and go as they please. I see my favorite spider in her web next to a broken statue of Don Quixote. I'm wearing three layers of clothes and a red stocking cap. I'm on the last chapter of *Elderhood* by Louise Aronson so I'll know what to do if I ever feel old.

You have to have a place like this. Describe it to me. I'll be right over.

Celebrate small pleasures. Everyday joys can last a lifetime.

Breakfast on Ice

So I'm sitting on one of those red swivel counter seats at this breakfast spot in Carson City. No one has chosen to sit next to me. I can't blame them. I'm going around and around and around at breakneck speed, or so it appears to me. I might be confused for an aging Peggy Fleming if it weren't for the fact that I'm slightly slouched, not twirling on silver skates and wearing a stained Wisconsin Badger T-shirt (not a fancy, pink skating outfit). Also, there's no hoppy-like music blaring out a familiar, seductive but family-appropriate tune.

For a few brief moments, I catch my bobbing head in the mirror behind the counter. And when the light shines just right from the circular pie case, I think to myself, Irene Kuhl's youngest boy could have been a late-blooming star of the Ice Capades.

This elation lasts for brief seconds.

Then I have a piece of coconut cream pie.

Simple Pleasures

What are some things that bring you joy?

Sherry speaks fondly of hanging laundry on the clothesline with her Aunt Janie. Sherry would hand her two clothespins at a time, and Aunt Janie would pin the sheets, work shirts and other freshly washed clothes against the blue Oklahoma sky. The sunshine and westerly winds would do their work, and the soft flapping of the drying clothes provided a peaceful backdrop to conversations about puppies, pancakes and other summer delights.

Right before I go to sleep, I often think of things that help me feel whole and happy. I conclude that it's the same things I enjoyed when I was 10: throwing and catching a football, reading a good short story or gently rubbing the ears of a sleepy dog.

What little things have brought you joy throughout your life? Are there places or smells or activities that bring a quiet glow of serenity to the rush of your day? You might be surprised at the profound happiness some of these simple pleasures still contain.

My Space

I've lived on the same property for almost 30 years. At the time, Sherry and I borrowed over our financial heads, but now we are blessed with a modest home on a great 10 acres attached to mountains that reach up toward Lake Tahoe.

The property was a lot like me when we first moved in. It offered little when it came to curb appeal. The land had a few dying trees, heaps of sagebrush, more foxtails than stars in the sky and a long, dusty driveway that served as a trail for bears and coyotes.

We worked the property every weekend, planting trees and seeding the sandy soil. We bought an old trailer and hauled sagebrush, weeds and stumps to the local dump. Looking back over the decades, I equate the transformation of our property to my own transformation. Personally, I was able to get rid of a lot of junk stored in my head and replace it with ambitious goals and pleasant thoughts.

Today, I am pleased with my space.

Roy M. Quick

I think everyone over 70 should have Roy M. Quick, my cat for almost two decades.

Let's face it, I'm a dog guy. My other two cats don't care a smidgen about what's going on in my life. They don't come when I call them. They stare at me from across the room and make me feel uncomfortable, like I've done some nasty deed.

Roy M. Quick is different. He comes when I call him and often when I don't. Roy is task-driven. He helps me shave each morning. He checks the temperature of the tap water and he paws my shaving cream to inspect its consistency.

Roy takes naps with me. He lies on my chest, puts a paw on each side of my face and matches the rate of his breathing to mine. And, in the mornings, I don't need an alarm clock. At 5:30 a.m. sharp, Roy sticks his wet nose in my ear.

When I'm losing at chess, which is often, one swish of Roy's tail sends pawns and knights flying off the board. I'm uncertain how Roy knows I'm losing, but the odds are in his favor.

Roy M. Quick reduces my blood pressure. He makes me smile. Roy listens to me on my bad days.

If you are over 70, find your Roy M. Quick.

My Daily Celebration

When I was a young man, I managed a Ramada Inn in Iowa. My boss, Reuben, lived in Denver and was an excellent mentor. One day, after I missed getting our cash to the bank two days in a row, I got a call from Reuben saying, "Don, the most important task you have is to get the money to the bank each day." I said, "Yes, sir."

Nearly 50 years later, most banking is now done electronically. However, I still drive down the block from our publishing company to our wonderful local bank, City National, and make the daily deposit.

It may be a foolish behavior in many people's eyes, but for me there is a broader lesson in play. I see the bank as the finish line for each day's corporate efforts. It's tangible proof that our staff has performed admirably. Too often, we don't take every opportunity to celebrate success. There is nothing as tangible as a bank deposit to show we are on the right track.

By the way, the fact that City National Bank has chocolate chip cookies in the lobby has nothing to do with my daily visits.

Otto

When you reach a certain age, the chair you sit in counts.

My favorite chair, Otto, is in the TV room. It's green and cushy. Otto rocks back a bit, and a foot rest automatically appears. But let's be clear—it's not a La-Z-Boy. I promised Sherry I'd never get one of those. The name doesn't suit me. Otto is a masculine, German name dating back to the seventh century.

Otto has magic powers. Each Saturday, when I clean up the room, I reach deep into the lining of my chair. I'm always rewarded by pulling out a quarter, or at least a dime or two. Often, Otto gives me a couple peanuts or a kernel of popcorn as a special treat.

That's not all. My chair can make time disappear. Just last night, at 9 o'clock sharp, Otto and I were meeting our civic duty by watching a political debate. The next minute, I look up at the wall clock and it's quarter past 11.

Also, it's a bit surprising that no one else sits in Otto. My family and friends choose the newer, less comfortable chairs in the room. Go figure!

I know the time is coming. Sherry has hinted this old, green chair doesn't fit into the room decor. She's invited me to join her tomorrow after work at a fancy Reno furniture store.

But Otto knows if he gets carried out of the TV room, I'll be sitting on him.

I'm proud to be a man who likes to soak.

Bubble Bath

It ticks me off when mental health experts use the bubble bath as an example of a reward or special treat. What's more, this message is often directed exclusively to women.

My bubble bath is an essential part of a full day. It's not a luxury or a reward. I do not need to earn it. My wife takes brief, spartan showers and attempts to shame me out of my chosen path to cleanliness. I will not be intimidated by my wife or self-help authors. I'm proud to be a man who likes to soak.

Over the years, I have embraced a number of habits that diverge from perceived masculine behavior. Way back as a kid on our football team, I liked to wear the uniform but hated to get hit. Safely running out of bounds was my major goal.

I like romantic comedies, sometimes referred to as chick flicks. I laughed out loud when Harry met Sally.

I love writing poetry. It's not very good, even by my own standards. I just enjoy putting my crazy thoughts into a lyrical form.

One great thing about aging is freedom to be who you wish with little concern for how others respond to your behavior. For most of us, it took many years to learn that others aren't paying as much attention as we thought they were.

I'm enjoying this aging stuff. One bubble bath at a time.

Billy Bragg teaching
Zack ball tricks

Listen to your animal pals.
They can teach you a bunch.

Pass It On

I count myself fortunate to have seen generations of dogs, the senior experienced canines passing on their personalities and responsibilities to the little tykes that follow.

The photo on the left is of Billy Bragg (black) mentoring Zack Adams (white) in the way of *Play ball*. It has been our pack's tradition for over 30 years. *Play ball* is one of the many ways our dogs train the humans in their lives (mainly Sherry and me) how to have fun while improving our physical and mental state.

As senior humans, we now have the responsibility and opportunity to pass along all the wonderful lessons we have learned to the younger generations who follow us.

Here are a few on my list I try to pass on:

Spend more time outside.

Follow your passion.

Cardboard boxes can be toys.

Open doors for others (and yourself).

Fetching Pleasure

For 30 years, my dogs have made me feel important. Often, I've had four at a time. All of them have always been thrilled to see me, even when I'm in a bad mood. People who are not fond of dogs tell me they only act that way because I feed them. I tell them they are nuts.

Over the years, many of my dogs chased every ball I threw. A few of them even returned the ball to me. They rarely do as I request, but that's okay. They are dogs, not indentured servants.

If you are aging and feel pangs of loneliness, I advise you to get a dog. I've had lots of nice neighbors but none of them have been so thrilled to see me come home.

Alice Pea Tucker

Until recently, Sherry and I had two cats, Roy M. Quick and Alice Pea Tucker. We got the two tabbies when they were just little puffs of orange motion. Living in the same old house for 18 years, they knew the inner workings of our home better than we did.

For many years, their "magic window" was opened early in the morning, and the two jumped out to play for precious minutes on the side of the house. As if trained by some cat whisperer (of course, there is no such person), they hopped back on the window sill in unison ready for a little canned tuna when it was time to come in. In the afternoons, when the sun heated up our hardwood floor under our bedroom window, the two of them curled up together and breathed as if they were one.

Roy M. Quick died a few months ago, and we buried him in the bird garden. For days, I watched Alice Pea roaming our house, checking in cupboards and closets looking for her pal. I opened the "magic window," but Alice Pea stayed on the window sill. Waiting. In the afternoons, she couldn't find the right sun-soaked spot on our hardwood floor. The tuna in the food tray stayed untouched.

Sherry and I held Alice Pea and gave her extra love, but for weeks her meows sounded more like moans. We knew we were no substitute for her lifelong buddy, Roy M. Quick.

But early this morning when I opened the "magic window," Alice Pea Tucker jumped off the window sill.

Aging comes with the pain of loss. There is no getting around it.

But time and love help the healing.

Amy Beth Baker

My name is Amy Beth Baker, I'm five years old and I'm a black German shepherd.

I am the guard dog for Sherry and Don and my pals, two white Swiss shepherds, who prefer to play more than protect. I stare down packs of coyotes, chase black bears off the property and inform roaming mountain lions to hunt elsewhere.

I don't allow humans to come through our front gate unless Sherry or Don officially let me know it's okay. Then I keep a wary eye on them. That is my job, and I do it well.

Don't get me wrong, I have a soft side. I particularly love Sherry. I'm often at her side getting appreciative pats on my head as we hike up the mountain. She likes to wrestle with me too. We roll around in the grass like a big battle is going on, and then I flop on my back, and Sherry rubs my belly.

Today I'm at my least favorite place, the animal hospital. I'm in lots of pain. They call it cancer. Sherry has tears in her eyes while she cradles my head as I go to sleep.

Note from Don: Amy Beth Baker taught us that it's not about how many years you live but how loyal and steadfast you are toward those you love.

Here's Amy Beth showing my grandson Nathan some affection

The Eternal Frog

"You're nuts," my surgeon neighbor said to me. "Frogs don't live for 15 years."

"Apples has, and he's as healthy as ever," I told him.

Apples is a cute little green frog that hangs out on top of the cabinet in my garage. Over the years, Sherry and I have provided him a mason jar lid pond, a heat lamp, plenty of green grass and lots of love. Actually, Apples most enjoys staying next to some rusted bolts, broken pliers and a yellow crayon, but I know he appreciates the pond when it gets really warm.

I check on him each morning before I go to work and look for him when I return home. Apples is an affluent frog and goes on lengthy vacations, sometimes for months. I don't worry. I just make sure his neighborhood stays in order, and Apples always shows up sooner or later.

My neighbor, the surgeon, is a busy man, but when he doubted the existence of Apples, I made him follow me to my garage. Thank goodness Apples was home lounging against the yellow crayon.

"Don, you need to get a life," he told me.

I don't think surgeons have time for frogs that live on and on.

It's okay. I do.

Rattlesnake Killer

My old boss Gordon told me that when someone is doing important work, don't bother them with the details.

Wyatt Blue was a great dog, a blend of German shepherd and Rugged Nevada.

Two decades ago when we hiked the Pine Nut Mountain Range, Wyatt Blue, our new puppy, came upon a big rattlesnake. He began to circle the snake one way and then another. I yelled and stomped my feet, attempting to divert Wyatt's attention and save his life.

Wyatt paid no attention and suddenly grabbed the rattler in the middle of his body and shook him violently. The snake's head flew off in one direction and his rattle in another.

This "important work" was repeated many times in Wyatt's lifetime. I didn't bother him again. I just watched him from a safe distance.

Now, I think of Wyatt when a senior employee of The Change Companies® takes off on a high-risk venture. I don't bother them with the details.

Dog Gone It

Yesterday was not a good day.

Here's how it went. I come home from work with hard copy pages for this book. I have a great editor who has taken around 150 pages and used Post-it notes to tag areas for further development. This project is moving along ahead of schedule.

My cell phone rings, and I walk into the house to take the call. Thirty minutes later, I step outside and my wonderful shepherd, Jody Beth, greets me at the door. She has a sheet of paper in her mouth. I look out on the yard, and hundreds of scraps of paper are on the ground or floating in the brisk afternoon breeze.

With a new right hip and a heavy heart, it takes me nearly an hour to pick up the scraps. Jody Beth follows me around as I bend over and attempt to match pages with Post-it notes that may provide clues to my creative efforts.

Jody Beth wants me to pet her. When I was a younger man, I would have shouted to make her feel guilty.

Today, I smile and thank Jody Beth for her artistic contributions.

Love is one of the greatest commodities on Earth.

The Art of the Smooch

Love comes in many forms.

Billy Bragg was our long-haired German shepherd who led his pack for many years. He loved us dearly and showed it by giving us kisses on the face. However, Billy never learned the "art of the smooch." He'd lead with his teeth. He made every effort to be gentle but German shepherd teeth are German shepherd teeth.

The nip marks on our noses and cheeks became marks of pride for both Sherry and me. The more scratches, the more proven love.

As I age, love is shown by family and friends in many ways. My grandchildren are specialists in the use of sarcasm and mimicry that can produce a little sting at first until I remember they are youthful displays of affection. My best friends do not allow truth or sensitivity to get in the way of a good story at my expense. They call it humor. I call it love.

Love is one of the greatest commodities on Earth. I'll take mine in any way I can get it.

I Command You

My German shepherds rarely follow my instructions. Simple orders like, "Don't chase the cat" or "Bring me the newspaper" are ignored. No matter how rational my commands, I get nothing but blank stares.

Trying to command behavior from others has never gotten me far. When my son and daughter were young, I attempted to enforce household rules and instruct what I wanted them to do. I knew my way of thinking was in their best interest. They didn't think so.

Later in life, without being solicited, I told friends they "must" stop smoking or "should" lose weight. My advice never moved them to change.

Now, having spent nearly 30 years studying behavior change, I know words like "must" or "should" have little to no influence on people's behavior. All change is self-change. I can support others by showing respect, offering compassion and placing confidence in their personal efforts. The choice is always theirs.

It's so much easier to know what is right than to practice it. Even today, my adult children chuckle when I lecture them on money management. My friends mock my "words of wisdom."

And my German shepherds continue to chase the cat.

Snoop

For several years, Sherry and I have enjoyed the company of Snoop, a gopher snake who looks like a huge rattler. When I first met Snoop, I nearly stepped on him—and he didn't like it. He scared me silly.

After my initial panic, Sherry and I observed that this mammoth snake had no rattle. We've had practice identifying snakes on desert hikes—but Snoop was by far the biggest. So, I slowly made peace with Snoop, and he's been slithering around our property ever since, minding his own business.

With similar markings, gopher snakes are easily confused with rattlers. They also hiss loudly, shake their tails and coil up when threatened. Gopher snakes are not harmful to humans—unless you count scaring people senseless.

I've misjudged the intentions of many people in my life based on their outward appearance. Individuals I thought were my friends caused me pain. And unique characters I thought were out to get me became my good friends.

Today, I lounge lazily in the front yard in my favorite chair. Snoop is also sunning himself.

Thank goodness we both took a closer look.

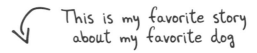
This is my favorite story about my favorite dog

Billy Bragg

Since dogs romp through life at a seven-to-one-year ratio to humans, there are many lessons they can teach us about living well. This is the story of Billy Bragg, our alpha German shepherd.

Even as a pup, Billy liked to separate from the pack and gallop after low-flying eagles. I always wondered if he was trying to chase them or join them.

Message for humans: There is a joy in pursuing lofty goals, even if those around you think you are a bit nuts.

Whenever our other three shepherds ran toward the front fence to scuffle with our neighbor's dogs, Billy Bragg would cut them off and assertively steer them back to the house.

Message for humans: Prompt action can avert serious problems. Leaders rush to the fire.

Late one night, a black bear entered our home through the living room window. Fortunately, Billy was there. He gave a growl so frightful that the bear jumped right back through the window and scampered up the mountainside.

Message for humans: Friends come to the rescue, even during dangerous times.

The day before Billy Bragg yielded to a fast-moving cancer, he joined us for a joyous winner's lap around his mountainous property. He led the pack as he always had, with authority and dignity.

Message for humans: Live your life to the fullest, finish your responsibilities and continue to love until the end.

Often, as we continue to hike with our three German shepherds up Billy Bragg's mountain, a single eagle flies low against the deep blue sky.

Message for humans: The spirit of life continues with the pack we leave behind.

Zack evolved from a scared,
moody pup into a trusted member
of the pack. Isn't that what we're
all shooting for?

Doggie Dreamland

When I can't go to sleep, I think of one of my faithful dogs of the past. Last night, it was Zackery Adams' turn to send me to dreamland.

Zackery was our "DSM-IV Dog" from a decade ago. As a puppy, he could have kept a psychiatrist busy for an entire career. He was super-sized, coming in around 120 pounds, but his feelings were fragile, easily hurt. If I didn't serve him first in the pack, he would sulk and not eat. If I petted one of his "brothers" before him, Zack curled up in his corner and did not budge. Our alpha shepherd, Billy Bragg, picked on Zack, attempting to cajole him out of his self-pity and into the family. Zack would have none of it.

The turning point arrived when Sherry and I brought home two new puppies, Mike and Buddy Rivers. Zack became the big, protective brother. He romped with the two tiny shepherds until all three collapsed in a big, furry bundle. Also, he became the favorite of our grandsons. Their fingertips could always find the top of Zack's head. He made sure they could go anywhere and return home safely. Zack was both playmate and protector to children too young to know danger or fear.

We only had Zack for eight great years. However, during that time, Zack evolved from a scared, moody pup into a trusted member of the pack.

And, as I awoke from my dream, I thought: Isn't that what we're all shooting for?

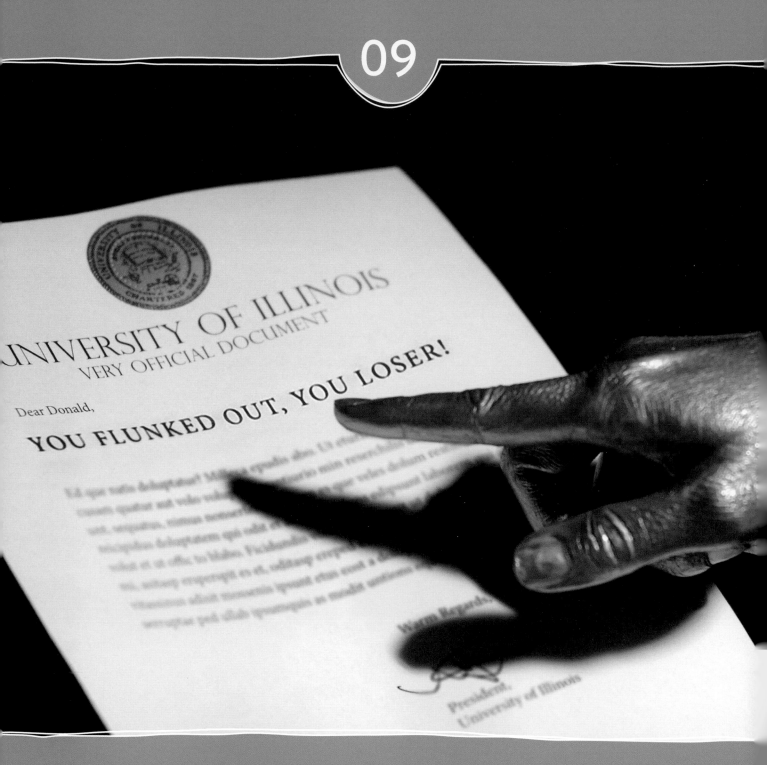

09

Focus on the positive.

Don't let bad things define you.

Flunking Out

Here's a fun way to bring a spring back in your step. Ask yourself, what was your most embarrassing moment in your past? How significant is it now? I've had a whole bunch of embarrassing moments, but the one that stands out most was at the end of my sophomore year at the University of Illinois.

I was sitting in an Urbana movie theater watching the James Bond movie "Goldfinger." In my back pocket was a formal letter from the University informing me I could not return for my junior year. In my mind it was saying, "Don, you stupid jerk, you flunked out." No doubt I deserved it. I was seldom in class—or even in the state of Illinois—during my sophomore year. I had more romantic and adventuresome activities on my agenda.

But all of a sudden, it hit me hard. I had two cans of Budweiser in my front coat pockets and a tub of buttered popcorn in my lap. They didn't help. I was crying, thinking about being a total failure and letting my parents down, being considered a fool by my friends who were going to prestigious universities and poor Don, having no idea where I could hide out for the rest of my life.

James Bond saved me. He was super cool and confident. I finished my beer and popcorn and walked out the door thinking I could only move up.

I did. Flunking out was the shot of failure I needed. For the most part, I've been riding high ever since.

Flunking out was the shot of failure I needed.

Failing for Good

I believe I should continue a lifelong habit well into my 70s: failure.

Failure has been my pathway to success and happiness over my many years. As a kid, I failed at being the starting quarterback. Several girls I wished to date, politely informed me of their lack of interest. A few years later, The University of Illinois requested that I discontinue the pursuit of my Accounting Degree. Over the decades, I started nearly a dozen corporations. A number of them went upside down in a hurry.

In all of these cases, I came out the other side a wiser and stronger person. I learned to accept failure with gusto, because I realized success was one step closer.

Goodness versus Indignities

I've been thinking about ups and downs across my life. It took me decades to share some of the "down" experiences with the people closest to me. What I've learned is, many of us suffered indignities while growing up.

I was sexually assaulted three times before reaching 12 years of age—once by a priest, another time by a football coach and a third time by a person I deeply trusted.

In each case, I stayed quiet. I was numb. I didn't understand.

Over the years, I tried to bury these events with heavy doses of alcohol and avoidance. I learned (the hard way) that such wounds demand attention to truly heal.

Now, at my ripe age, I look back at these dark memories and accept them as part of my story line, woven into the fabric of what makes me me.

I wish I had not experienced these cruel acts, but they do not define me. One of the beauties of living a full life is the opportunity to rebound, to work through personal pain and tap into the love and kindness that are all around.

Life comes with its share of indignities and goodness.

In my mind, the goodness has won out big time.

"You decide
what is a weed
and what is
a flower."

Life's Garden

Antonio and I had a failure to communicate.

He spoke Spanish and very little English. I spoke English and freshman high school Spanish.

It was over 25 years ago, and Antonio came over to help me bring our untamed yard under control. He was the neighborhood expert gardener. I was a sales guy.

It took weeks for Antonio's simple instruction to sink into my head. In broken English, he told me over and over, "You decide what is a weed and what is a flower. Pull, by the roots, what you see as a weed. Water and love what you see as a flower."

Sherry and I look at our yard today. It has huge, flowering weeds, patches of real grass and funny looking blue and yellow flowers (maybe flowers). We love it all. It's ours.

Reflecting back, I now realize Antonio's gardening advice had broader application. In my life as a whole, if I had consistently pulled all my prickly weeds by the roots and generously watered the magnificent opportunities that came my way, my life's landscape might be even more spectacular than it is today.

Scentless

Last week, I placed a big, black bag of smelly garbage from home in the back of Blue, my faithful Suburban. I planned to drop it off at the big waste bin at our warehouse, safely away from people's noses.

I got sidetracked and spent the whole day at my office. When I finally returned to my car, the putrid odor permeated the entire vehicle. Of course, I dumped my trash immediately. However, the pungent smell stayed in Blue and engaged my nostrils for a couple days afterward. It finally dawned on me I needed to do a thorough scrub to be totally free of my trash.

This experience got me thinking about all the garbage I've carried around in my mind over the years. Some of it I just let sit there, long after it had done its damage. The weight it placed on my spirit detracted from the joy that was waiting for me. Often, my own cleanup simply had to do with thoroughly forgiving myself, making any appropriate amends and moving on with a positive and odor-free mindset.

He Went to Paris

I have a favorite song. It was patched together by Jimmy Buffett, inspired by the life of a one-armed pianist, Eddie Balchowsky. The song was released in 1973. I discovered it many years later—and rediscovered it a few days ago.

I love it because it tells a life story. It starts with a young man "looking for answers to questions that bothered him so." As his life fills up, he sticks his questions in the attic, only to explore the answers in his 80s.

I'm deeply touched by the lyrics, and I can't quite figure out why. Maybe I hear pieces of many people's lives in this one beautiful song.

In the end, the man turns to Buffett and sums up his existence this way, "Jimmy, some of it's magic, some of it's tragic, but I had a good life all the way."

I hope, when I'm 86, I can have a similar answer to "questions that bother me so."

If you haven't heard this song, find it and play it... a life captured in one song.

Return of Augie the Angel

What's the most important message I ever received?

It was from Augie, my clumsy guardian angel, who chose to join me on a hike to Virginia City. Augie thinks he knows so much more than I do, and at times, he can be a bit self-righteous—but I guess angels have their reputations to uphold.

It was over 10 years ago, and I was on the hike to clear my mind. Life's issues were crowding out some of the joy in my life. I had some serious health issues I needed to deal with. My company was going through a transition and I felt insecure. I had just lost one of my favorite dogs to a fast-moving cancer.

Augie was having a hard time keeping up, even when he attempted to put his underdeveloped wings into action. I turned around and said, "Augie, life isn't going my way. You are a total flop in protecting me from all this bad stuff."

Augie, somewhat out of breath, replied, "You are in charge of your own life—no one else is. Your health issues are of your own making, as is the state of your company. Billy Bragg (my dog) brought you eight years of pure love and devotion. Celebrate his life and quit feeling sorry for yourself."

I responded, "You make it sound like I'm totally responsible for all the stuff that happens to me. Aren't you here to make me happy and content?"

I looked behind me, and Augie had vanished. I looked ahead and saw Virginia City and the rest of my life in front of me.

A Poem

I'm so sorry, but I've decided to include a poem in this chapter. Very few people really read and enjoy poems, but this one I wrote many years ago helped me age out of my stupidity.

SHOWDOWN

Rigorous Honesty
dressed in white,
sun at his back,
rode into town.

My gang
took cover
in the wasted crannies of my mind.

False Pride
strutted on the rooftop.

Fear
hid under a wagon.

Procrastination
lingered by the saloon.

Deception
looked unarmed
but wasn't.

Guns blazed.
Good prevailed.

Rigorous Honesty
saved my town.

St-stuttering

One of the greatest gifts I received as a kid was my stuttering talent.

At times I could not get out a single word, much less a coherent sentence or two.

I drove my loving father, Vern, nuts. He'd counsel me, "Don, think about what you want to say before you begin to speak." I always knew what I wanted to say. I just couldn't get the words out.

So why do I now consider stuttering a gift?

It made me look inward, to create in my mind what I could not express with words.

I became sensitive to others who had all kinds of problems. I found myself rooting for them as they coped with arrogant kids and bullies.

When I was quite young, I started to write and stick my stories and poems in a secret treasure box. I still do.

I learned to be resilient.

I listened more than most kids my age.

I was in my late teens before a smart friend told me I should practice stuttering on purpose. I kind of enjoyed it. This simple tip gave me considerable control over my speech patterns.

Every now and then, I still stutter on purpose just to tick off someone who is bugging me.

After all, I don't want to lose such a wonderful gift.

Remember the Good

On two occasions last month, I heard friends of mine, both in their 70s, beat themselves up over poor choices they made many years ago.

As they shared dark secrets from decades earlier, I thought about the weight they had been carrying with no particular benefit to themselves or the people close to them.

I'm no expert in such matters, but I very much want to give them the power to let go of their guilt and remorse. Maybe it's a failing of my own, but I'm pretty good at forgiving myself for my many screw-ups and (hopefully) learning a useful lesson I can apply in the future.

One trick that works for me is to make amends as quickly as possible. And I make them as briefly and directly as I can. I don't try to recreate or explain the circumstances of my poor behavior. I listen closely to what the other person wants me to hear. I make eye contact and say, "I'm sorry." Then my job is to make certain my future actions support the substance of my apology.

That's it. In my eyes, when you are in your 70s, remember all the good things you have accomplished. While you're at it, look toward future happiness by providing love and compassion to those around you.

10

Be courageous.

Step bravely into the next stage of life.

Happy Endings

If you are like me, and you are in the last few chapters of a book you are really gobbling up, you have mixed feelings about bringing it to a conclusion. You may glance back at the former chapters, smiling at the characters, entanglements and adventures that caught your interest and imagination.

I'm exactly at that point in the book I keep in my head, "The Misadventures and Wonderful World of Me." I can turn this book on its edge and see the bookmark is over three-fourths of the way to the back cover. I don't have the foggiest idea how it will end. There are still a few story lines that need to come together, and the author (that would be me) knows I'm not much for unfulfilled culminations. I wish I could make the ending move more slowly, but the pages are flipping by at a more accelerated rate.

Read on, Don. Finish it up with gusto.

Who knows, decades from now, a grandson might be sharing the final chapter of my life with his youngest daughter. She may laugh with delight, saying, "I'm glad it had such a happy ending."

Words from Vern

My family got our first TV when I was about seven.

It had a knob to change channels. There were three choices.

Often the screen looked snowy, with wavy lines moving from top to bottom.

My father, Vern, bought rabbit ears and moved them all around. The fuzzy snow and wavy lines persisted.

Nothing worked, and Vern said words he did not want me to hear.

Many, many years later I have a brand-new TV with over 120 channels to choose from.

Last night, during a crucial football game, the whole screen went dark: no fuzzy snow, no wavy lines, no rabbit ears to play with.

Alone, in the dark, I repeated the words my father said long ago.

Did I mention my TV has over 120 channels?

Beating the Average

I know it's sick to think this way, but I can't help myself.

About six months ago, I started looking at various tables representing life expectancy. It's like I want to make sure I beat the survival average for my gender and nationality. There are many ways the experts can slice the numbers. I'm either supposed to be dead by the time I'm 76.1 (right around the corner), or I stay upright until 92.4 (generations away).

Don's sick brain talking to Don: "Wouldn't it be a poor showing if you dropped dead before your time is due? You better eat more vegetables, quit stressing out over the little stuff and find a better mantra to chant while meditating."

Don's even sicker brain continues to talk to Don: "Maybe you should be more proactive and make a list of all the men you know in your age group who you think may outlast you. Then you can subtly recommend high-risk behaviors to them. "Hey Joe, I hear cliff diving is a fun activity." "Peter, did you know the new high fat, high sugar diet will make you look years younger?" "George, how fast can that new car of yours go around Deadman's Curve?"

Then, when I pass at a respectable age, beating the odds by a dozen years, the few friends left to attend my funeral will remark to each other, "Don was a peculiar and insecure man. It's too bad he lived so long."

The great thing about getting older is that you don't lose all the other ages you've been.

-Madeleine L'Engle

Old Man

Madeleine makes an excellent point. So often, I see an older person at the airport or at the grocery store, and that's all I see. The person looks wrinkled, slow and seemingly lost.

But that ninety-year old has so many stories to tell. I'll bet he was once a third grader anxious for the recess bell to ding. Perhaps he was a soldier protecting his homeland. My guess is, he fell in love and married and had children, then grandchildren, then great-grandchildren. Think of all the times he laughed. By this time, he has felt the pain of losing close friends and relatives who shaped his life as he shaped theirs. My hunch is, he has a favorite song in his heart.

Yet, today I look at him, and all I see is an old man.

Then, I study the backs of my own hands. I see little cracks and faint brown spots I never noticed before. They make me smile. I also remember the sweet sound of the recess bell.

The Widowmaker

I'm in the lobby of a small hotel in Dallas when I feel sudden discomfort. A moment later, I'm sprawled on the carpet, my chest exploding in ripples of pain. I see people watching me with curiosity and concern. I hear a siren. The ambulance takes me to the University of Texas Southwestern Medical Center a few blocks away. I think it's a long, long ride.

Dr. Aslan Turer is on duty. He grabs my hand. I close my eyes tight and see an oval shaped portal with hues of soft yellow and blue inviting me through. I feel peace. I feel free.

(Fact: I have a Proximal LAD Lesion, appropriately called the Widowmaker, with less than a 6% survival rate.)

I open my eyes uncertain of where I am. For a moment, or maybe several minutes, my mind floats across my life. My past screw-ups fade and drop from my consciousness. Only my goodness comes through, not in specific detail, more like a warm blanket wrapped softly around my entire body.

Things become clearer. I recognize I'm in a recovery room at a hospital in Dallas. A day goes by slowly and then a young stranger, a kid, strolls in my hospital room and stares at me. He says, "Donald, you have a strange sense of humor."

I ask, "Who are you?"

I almost lost my ability to age.

He smiles, "We met in the emergency room. I'm Aslan Turer, and you whispered funny, self-deprecating stories while I was putting in your stent."

Turns out Aslan is a superstar surgeon, having got a fellowship at Duke University Medical Center. He is a national leader in understanding and fixing hearts that have gone wacko, and I must be a guy who talks too much all of the time...

Looking back, it is apparent I almost lost my ability to age. However, I was given two great gifts. The first is obvious, I've been blessed with nearly five additional years on earth to play and work and love and, hopefully, more years to come.

The second gift is why I feel this life story is worth sharing. When I came close, or actually traveled, to my next destination, I did not fear, nor did I experience shame for past indiscretions. I had a feeling of peace and anticipation as I approached my portal.

For those who know me well, you are aware I made plenty of poor choices and I inflicted harm and unnecessary pain on others. Yet, I attempted to atone for these behaviors by doing good stuff, although I continue to mess up from time to time.

So if a guy like me can feel so darn content when close to death, all of you are going to have it made when your time comes near. Enjoy each day of aging, and spread the love.

Wisdom from Carl

Carl Jung is one of my three favorite psychologists. What he said about aging has got to be true.

"A human being would certainly not grow to be 70 or 80 years old if this longevity had no meaning for the species to which it belongs. The afternoon of human life must also have a significance of its own and cannot be merely a pitiful appendage to life's morning."

I can't write as eloquently as Jung, but I'm old enough to know what he was talking about. As I age, each additional day I have on earth is a gift, but the significance of those days is determined by the little choices I make.

What's Old?

When can I earn the right to be called an old guy? That magic age keeps creeping up higher and higher.

Back in high school, I thought my parents were pretty darn old. Why else would they be watching "The Lawrence Welk Show"?

My mind changed when I approached 40 and thought of being able to retire at 60. I said to myself, "In another 20 years, I will quit working, kick back and enjoy doing nothing like all the old people do."

Now, still working at 74, I question whether I qualify to be called an elderly gentleman.

In Nevada, I look around me at people of all ages. In our state, 74% of the population is under 65. Percentagewise, the best state to be around folks over 65 is Maine, closely followed by Florida. Would I be better off moving there?

Maybe I'll reach old age when I'm 100. If so, I should move back to the state I was in: Iowa. It is one of three states (Connecticut and Hawaii being the others) that would give me the best shot at enjoying the company of other centenarians.

Sherry says I shouldn't waste my time thinking about all this aging stuff. Besides, a rerun of "The Lawrence Welk Show" is about to start.

The Titanium Man

I just wasn't hip for around 74 years. But all of that changed in 2019. My original hips kept me from showing off my best dance moves. They also limited my ability to run, then kept me from Tahoe Rim Trail hikes and finally, made it painful to just walk a block.

So in May, I decided to have a total hip replacement on my right side, replacing my arthritic, old hip with a shiny, new, titanium one. My surgeon, Chad (think Doogie Howser), looked far too young to be entrusted with my hip, but I appreciated his no-frills demeanor.

Two months later, my right side was doing great. But my left side was really hurting. I could barely walk. In November, I called up Doogie (I mean Chad) and asked if he had another titanium hip handy. He did. So on Dec. 4, I went back in to have him do his stuff again.

It's January now. I can move with little pain. Sherry informs me it's the first time I've ever walked a straight line (exactly what does she mean by such a remark?).

From now on, I'm the swift and nimble Titanium Man, keeping peace and order on the Tahoe Rim Trail.

I wish it had worked out... my back got in the way.

More Roundabouts

I'm getting too old to accept all these newfangled ideas.

Early in my life, streets that bumped into other streets created an intersection. If the two streets were not busy ones, drivers were smart and courteous enough to figure out which vehicle or buggy had the right of way.

If one street handled more traffic than the other, stop signs were put up on the less busy street. If both streets carried a bunch of vehicles, a four-way stop was installed. Often, it's difficult to figure out who should go first. I've seen fights break out.

Traffic lights became the next big thing. Colored lights and arrows tell drivers when they can go—or must stop. Yellow means uncertainty, testing each individual's level of risk taking.

Some great brain came up with the idea of roundabouts. This is when all cars, coming from any direction, drive around a tiny circle.

The Departments of Transportation put out "scientific studies" showing that roundabouts reduced accidents by 37%. Yeah, right.

My little town of Carson City has gone nuts. They are installing roundabouts at an alarming rate.

I'm too old for all this progress.

If I have my way, I will fall off my stool at an ice cream shop and go right to heaven.

Dying Well

It's not in my strategic plan to drop dead for many years. Still, achieving a good death is something I ponder.

So far, I have been present while six individuals have died. Four of them passed peacefully. It was as if I was reading the final chapter of a beautifully written book. All four had prepared for their exits. In three cases, people who loved the person were present for emotional support. The fourth one died unexpectedly but had led such a spectacular life, I think I saw a contented smile on her face when she took her last breaths.

The other two deaths I witnessed were painful to watch. I saw desperation. I saw anger. Most of all, I saw terror in each of their faces.

What makes the difference in people's final chapter? I've given this a lot of thought. I've also read the ideas of many experts on what makes for a peaceful end.

If I have my way, I will fall off my stool at an ice cream shop and go right to heaven.

In any case, I believe I will die a happy man if I do the following five things:

1. I demonstrate kindness to people I love. And those I don't.

2. I continue to get to know me better—and make wise decisions based on what I find out.

3. I do the best with what I've got, and I don't fret over what I'm missing.

4. I don't take myself too seriously. After all, nobody else does.

5. I always wear clean underwear, just like my mother taught me (translation: maintain a sense of humor).

Whatever happens, I am determined to write my final chapter through actions that bring joy to me and those around me.

Final Words

Frank Tate—the kindest, brightest man I've ever known—was born in Tuscola, Illinois, in 1916. He died comfortably, peacefully, in Carson City, Nevada, on Dec. 24, 2004. His final words to me were, "Don, quit fussing over me and get about your duties."

Frank was an educator of the highest order. In over 40 years, I never heard him say a discouraging word about anyone. Ever. His gentle guidance, often delivered with humor, provided a foundation of knowledge and confidence to hundreds of young people trying to find their way in the turbulent 1960s and beyond.

I still miss Frank, particularly on disquieting days. Then I reflect on his final message to me. We all have the opportunity and the responsibility to "get about our duties" and play a positive role in the lives of those around us.

Frank's spirit lives on.

I just need to get busy doing the important things in my life.

The man I admired most. I miss his love and wisdom.

"Don, quit fussing over me and get about your duties."

Don the Undone

As I'm getting into my senior years, it dawns on me what I wish to put on my tombstone.

"Here lies Don. He's undone."

When it's time for me to go to heaven, or at least to some spectacular spot, I know I'll be in the midst of doing a whole bunch of things that will be left unfinished.

The whole mindset of wrapping things up as one ages has been totally lost on me. Instead, I keep unwrapping wonderful adventures that I know will never reach the finish line. In fact, I think I was born and groomed for starting things—and I'm not very good at finishing them.

A few examples:

I want to pull every foxtail weed in my yard and get the entire root of those darn suckers.

I want Carson City to be appreciated for its great contribution to wild west American history and share it with children from around the world. I still dream of ways of making that happen.

I want to hike the Pacific Crest Trail. *I'll meet you there at Marlette Lake!*

I want fearful individuals who have fallen into a hole, whether due to mental health issues, addiction or brushes with the law, to recognize they possess the fortitude to make their lives more meaningful and joyous. It's up to them to make it happen.

I want to look everyone I love in the eyes and tell them how fortunate I've been to know them.

I want to consume a large chocolate marshmallow milkshake without feeling any sense of guilt.

Liminal Space

I've been reading a bunch about this whole aging thing. Also, I have about 20 friends who are marching along with me toward their 80s and above.

While journaling last evening, an interesting observation hit me.

One way of looking at aging is, we all are no longer [fill in the blank, such as employed, married, mobile, healthy] and we are moving toward whatever it is that will define the rest of our lives.

Richard Rohr defines this as liminal space, "a sacred space where the old world is able to fall apart, and a bigger world is revealed."

I'm scaring myself. I sound too highfalutin. I apologize.

All I'm saying is, as we get older, lots of what we are used to starts to disappear and often we are uncomfortable or uncertain about what is coming next.

I recommend hanging out with the discomfort. There's something there.

I don't like
friends dying
on me.

Missing in Action

I don't like friends dying on me. Didn't they realize how much I counted on them?

This has been a tough year. I count four important people in my life who took off—most of them without any notice at all.

When close friends or relatives die, no one is there to take their specific place in my inner circle. It isn't like trading in an old, reliable car for a newer model. Each close friend is unique, one of a kind.

And here is where I am so selfish. My best buddies leave this earth with a special appreciation and understanding of me. They knew me, my warts, my failures and accomplishments. It was impossible for them to bequeath that special knowledge and love to another human being.

The good part is, I have cherished memories of them to ruminate on each day. And no one can steal those away from me.

You guys went missing. But you are still with me.

Kevin

One of my heroes had a stroke. I've known him nearly a lifetime.

Kevin lovingly told me many years ago to quit talking so much about myself and my fabricated success stories. He said to stay quiet and listen to the wisdom and beauty of others. At the time, I did not have the courage to do that. For years, I kept blathering.

Now, my friend is courageously working at regaining his ability to fully function. During this time of challenge, he is mentoring me in ways he will never know. When he is asked what year it is, Kevin smiles before taking a wild stab at it. He's off by decades. At lunch, when trying to figure out the real purpose of a fork and spoon, he thanks the nurse for being so patient.

Decades ago, Kevin owned a huge corporate space in a major international corporation.

Now, Kevin owns another space. Today he's even more my hero.

Death, My Friend

My friends and colleagues who have reached the age of 70 or beyond appear to have little interest in the topic of death.

I'm a different kind of guy. It might be because twice in my last eight years, I thought I was making a grand exit. For me, neither time was a scary experience. I don't want to say it was fun, like going to a birthday party, but it was okay. The warm glow of acceptance kept me from freaking out.

Since my encounters, I've read three outstanding books on the topic: *When Breath Becomes Air* by Paul Kalanithi, *The Art of Dying Well* by Katy Butler and *Farewell* by Edward Creagan. I thought, why not take an interest in something I know will take place in my lifetime?

This is how I think about death today—a kind and loving friend waiting patiently at my back door. Death allows me to come and go as I please through my front door: going to work, playing with my dogs, embracing loved ones. It may be next week or 20 years from today before I hear my back door gently open.

When it happens, I'm going to give my patient friend a warm greeting.

Very Happy?

In a recent study by the University of Chicago, Americans were asked if they were very happy. Only 14% answered "yes." That's a 17% drop from a 2018 survey and the lowest ever recorded. Using my mathematical wizardry, I recognized that means more than four out of five of us are less than very happy.

Why we are not very happy remains a bit of a puzzle. Based on other findings, it appears that financial status is not the answer, nor race, age or where we happen to live.

As for me, I'm very, very happy. I'm blessed. I have a loving wife who only drives me nuts on occasion. I continue to banter with and love close friends who put up with me. I go to work each day and get immersed in projects I find challenging and worthy. I have four dogs who find me very desirable.

For all of us older folks, I recommend focusing on the simple things that bring us pleasure. I try to stay away from political and financial battles. I focus on flowers, cloud formations, and family and friends who bring me joy.

Just last evening, I looked up and saw a cloud formation that looked like an old locomotive blowing out white puffs of smoke.

I thought it might be taking a person to heaven. That made me very happy.

As for me,
how could I be happier?

Expiration Date

I read somewhere: "Enjoy life now. It has an expiration date."

What if a tall stranger in a tan trench coat slipped me a note saying, "Your expiration date is tomorrow"?

What would I do differently?

My first thought is, "By golly, I'd better get busy."

Doing what?

My lawyer would say, "Don, get your legal affairs in order."

My accountant would say, "Don, did you pay your quarterly property tax?"

Sherry would ask me for a longer hug in the morning.

As for me, I'd want to think very deeply about the meaning of my life.

Then I'd fall down purposefully on the cool, green grass in my backyard.

My four white shepherds would rush over and jump on me.

Ahh... Lord, I'm ready.

Health or Wealth

As a kid, I got so annoyed with my mother, Irene, always yakking, "If you don't have your health, nothing else matters." I'd wait 10 seconds and my dad, Vern, would pipe in, "And it doesn't hurt to have a bunch of money in the bank."

Now, many years later, I've had a taste of both. Over the last six years, I've had a LAD heart attack, two back surgeries and a hip replacement. In fact, I go in for a second hip replacement in December. I'm thinking, "Gosh mom, you may have dished out some wisdom in your yakking."

On the other end of my parental guidance, Vern also had a point. I've been broke a few times. It changes your priorities. It causes emotional pain. Presently, I experience a level of wealth that many do not attain. A modicum of wealth takes a number of issues off the table.

This is what I've found to be the bottom line. Today, my physical condition is quite limited. I have chronic pain. I can't hike except to the bathroom. Yet, I can do many things that bring me joy.

On the other hand, I have a measure of wealth which allows me to do stuff I only dreamed of in my younger years. Yet, wealth comes with responsibility. How do I use it to serve others?

So, at 74, do I think the ultimate parental wisdom rested with Vern or Irene? An easy way out would be to say, do the best you can with what you have.

Yet, truth be told, I've been accused of being a momma's boy. I'd take health over wealth any day of the week.

An Auction

Sherry and I were walking our way through the county roads of Iowa going from the northern border of the state to the south when we came upon a farm auction not far out of the little town of Boone. Pickup trucks and dusty cars lined either side of the road, and the miked voice of an auctioneer floated above the rows of corn.

I spotted the Nelsons, husband and wife, on the front porch of the farmhouse their grandfather had built, watching as neighbors and strangers grouped around the various tables of goods for sale in boxes organized by category. Kitchen supplies on one table, bedding, towels and curtains on another. Everything must go.

Straw hatted veterans were inspecting the tractors and balers in the large red barn. Others milled among the livestock patting the flanks of mares and observing the dozen or so cows grazing on the Iowa grass.

The local bank could wait no longer. When the sun set that evening, a lifetime had been sold.

Sherry and I held hands as we slowly walked away.

When the sun set that evening, a lifetime had been sold.

Talk to the Old Guy

My guess is, most people over 70 have times when they are struggling a bit.

I've hit a few weeks of this. Nothing big, mind you. Just little, nagging medical issues and personal decisions I need to make. I keep pushing them off for another day. Then another week or so. They linger in my mind and make me a bit anxious.

I went for a walk in a beautiful park with a friend who happens to be a psychiatrist and asked for advice. She said, "What would be the recommendations from an 85-year-old Don to help out the 75-year-old Don?" (I assumed she knew I was the 75-year-old Don in this scenario) Then she left me alone by a big pine tree for 15 minutes.

When my friend returned, she asked me if I had received sound advice.

I said, "Yes, the old guy gave me some straight answers. He's so much smarter than me."

If you get in one of those funks, I'd recommend you seek advice from the you 10 years down the road.

Last Quarter

Let's pretend we all are going to live to be 100 years old. And we wish to break our full lives into quarters and define each quarter with a single word. What would those four words be?

I'm approaching the end of my third quarter, so my first three words are based on personal experience and self-reflection:

First quarter: Discover

Second quarter: Execute

Third quarter: Contribute

But what about the fourth quarter? The one I hope is coming my way.

I'm stumped. What word best describes this final quarter?

Your life has little to do with what you throw away. It's all about what you choose to keep.

The Keepers

While moving toward retirement, I've been throwing away a lot of my old stuff.

I don't consider myself a pack rat. Still, this has not been an easy task for me. Most of my things can be dumped without any regrets. However, I get these emotional tugs from some of the strangest items.

Here are just a few examples of my keepers:

My mother's dictionary.

My third-place bowling trophy from eighth grade, which I used to fix that toilet. The engraved plaque is seriously rusted.

A note from Mary Walsh, the first girl I kissed when I was 13. It has a cute picture of a kitten on the outside. Inside, written in pencil, is the message: "Sorry, I don't like you anymore."

My dad's watch, which he gave me the week before he died in 1999. It stopped working years ago. The jeweler told me it can't be fixed, but I swear I can still hear it tick late at night.

A June 1976 handwritten note from "Gwen" Brooks (a great poet) telling me she was sending my "vital and memorable work" to Ann Harris, her editor at Harper and Row.

An August 1976 typed reply from Harper and Row's Ann Harris, informing me my poetry wasn't up to their standards.

I have a recommendation for my elderly friends who might wish to empty their drawers and closets.

Your life has little to do with what you throw away. It's all about what you choose to keep.

Decision Maker

It was a muggy July night in 1958 when I learned my life was about to change in a big way. I was walking back from playing basketball at Brookside Park in Ames, Iowa, and my Dad picked me up.

Three blocks went by in silence. Then, about two blocks from home, my Dad said, "We're moving to Chicago." That was it, like he was saying we were having roast beef for dinner.

Now, in my mid-70s, I look back on some of the huge decisions that altered my life. In the case of moving from Iowa to Chicago, the decision was made by my parents, but it altered my life forevermore. In adulthood, most of the big decisions in my life were made by me, and I reaped the benefits or paid the consequences of my choices.

That got me thinking, so I made a list of the 10 biggest decisions in my life so far. Did I make them, or did someone else? My score so far is seven (me) versus three (others).

Why is this important today? Because my guess is, my life has one or two big decisions coming up. I'd like to be the one who makes them.

Conclusion

Thank you for letting me share segments of my aging story with you. Perhaps little pieces of it will be helpful in your unique and worthy pathway of aging.

I'd love to learn more about your own life's adventures. I'm confident you have much to teach me. If you get in the mood, I can be reached through The Change Companies®' website, changecompanies.net, or shoot me an email at dkuhl@changecompanies.net.

Acknowledgments

The creation of this book has been so much fun. And what a remarkable collaboration by so many!

Three talented members of The Change Companies®' creative team played a major role in making this book come together.

 Jenni Hodges is my editor and so much more. She lets me know when my Aging blogs are good... and those that need to disappear. Often, Jenni cleverly adds and deletes words and phrases to my writings as if I will never notice the edits. I notice but say nothing so I can take full credit for the finished work.

Christine Kegel brings her flair for graphics and color to all that we do at The Change Companies®. She volunteered to help give this book its personality. She has the talent to even make me look good.

 Valerie Bagley helped with the original concept and provided the organizational structure for the book. Valerie knows me well and used all of her wisdom in positive psychology to gently guide me in the right direction.

I receive inspiration from our team at The Change Companies® each work day. This group of creative professionals practices the principles of positive behavior change in their personal lives as they create products that serve millions of individuals around the world.

Much of this book is based on my blog, *Aging Monday, Wednesday, Friday*. Over the last couple of years, many readers have responded with their support and their own stories that have touched my heart. I would not have had the courage to write this book if it had not been for their kind support and words of wisdom. This exchange made it abundantly clear we all have so much in common. Stories of my life are often common threads of the aging experiences we all share. In many ways, this book is about all of us.

Of course, this book is about my life's adventures and misadventures. As is true in your life, hundreds of individuals have influenced my journey, most of them leading me in a positive direction. I owe them my appreciation for helping me get this far.

My wife, Sherry, is my inspiration. She has helped shape my story (and in turn, this book) for nearly four decades. My sisters, Connie and Kelly, have been with me for a lifetime and continue to pop into my life in positive ways. I love them so much. My two adult children, Jeff and Kate, also add special meaning. I am humbled by their success as parents, as professionals and as just plain good folks. I try to take as much credit as I can for the way they have aged.

And thanks to you for reading *Changing with Aging*. It completes the circle of this meaningful adventure.